All About the Spirit World

Tony Scazzero

ISBN: 1-4791-8497-7
ISBN-13: 9781479184972

Cover image depicts Isaiah 11:6 metaphor for heaven:

"The wolf also shall dwell with the lamb, and THE LEOPARD SHALL LIE DOWN WITH THE KID; and the calf and the young lion and the fatling together; and a little child shall lead them."

Artwork by Hannah Selig Scazzero
www.hannahscazzero.com

Dedicated to:
Heavenly Mother and Heavenly Father

Contents

Preface

All About the Spirit World summarizes the main concepts about life after death. How odd that even in today's technologically advanced society, most people are unaware of what their future will be like they leave the earth. It is my desire to enlighten people spiritually by increasing their knowledge of the spirit world.

Also, this would greatly reduce the task of those who need to explain to newcomers where they are when they arrive in the spirit world.

Tony Scazzero

INTRODUCTION

Death is the predictable end to life on earth. The hard fact is that everyone will face death sooner or later. But what happens when we die? This subject has always challenged mankind. Since the dawn of mankind, the human mind has pondered death, searching for answers to its mysteries.[1] Yet quite a few people prefer to leave the whole subject of the afterlife alone. Despite plentiful evidence and testimonies, the majority of people are unsure what awaits them after death. Even though the process of dying is expected from birth, most people have lived in ignorance about its consequences. Any encounter with death brings an uneasy feeling of one's own mortality. Whenever death does revisit, there is another futile attempt to understand its significance. Does life continue into another world? If there is another world, what is it like? It is all too confusing. Eighty percent of the world's population does not know about the spirit world.[2]

The thought of the hereafter often causes apprehension and even fear. Some even connect death with the likes of zombies, vampires, evil spirits, ghosts and the grim reaper. The issue of death has strongly influenced man's outlook on life. Death has been a great inspiration for poets, musicians, artists, writers and philosophers. Yet very few people look forward to life in the next world. Contrary to popular belief, life after death should not bring despair but a great happiness. It is similar to when a baby leaves the realm of water in the mother's womb and is greeted by family and friends. The baby inside the mother doesn't know there is another world waiting outside. Likewise, earthly death is not the ending but a new start to life.

The most peculiar thing is that when most people die, they do not comprehend that they are dead. Upon passing away, nearly everyone is astonished to find they are living in another dimension. Many people leave the earth with no knowledge of the most important part of the universe—the spirit world.[3] Yet, after death they still continue to experience the same consciousness including all their senses.

All the knowledge, experience and personality of the physical body are inherited by the spirit body. Not only that, but their spirit man is identical in appearance to the physical man and lives for eternity in the invisible world after leaving the physical body.[4]

Since most people are not taught to deal effectively with death, even more grief occurs when it is actually confronted. Denial of the afterlife leaves one without the necessary training needed to do well in the next world. When someone thinks that the physical life is all they have, they are literally living only half the life they could be living. The end result of this ignorance is an intimidating fear of death. If only the laws and conditions of spirit life were universally diffused throughout the earth world, what a wealth of difference it would make.[5]

Whether it is a test at school, shopping to cook, training for the military or researching a major purchase, preparation time is always necessary. When someone plans for a long trip to a new or unfamiliar destination, they get organized to the best of their ability. They book room reservations, learn about the popular destinations, the exchange rate and the language. Families plan for their vacations months, sometimes years in advance. No one makes an expedition, especially to an unknown land, without anticipating and preparing for every possible need and contingency.[6] Ironically, most people will prepare thoroughly before any earthly trip, yet will pay little or no attention for the trip to infinity and beyond. For most people the only preparation for death is making a will, getting their worldly affairs in order and possibly a last minute prayer of remorse. Although dying is a known conclusion, the majority throughout the world do not make plans for life after death. In fact, many give it little or no thought until it is too late. To this day there exist very few people who are spiritually awake to the world before death, and even fewer who have any accurate grasp at all of human life beyond physical death.[7] As a result, nearly everybody is unprepared for the greatest journey of their entire life. Consequently, some spirit people could end up in an undesirable location or position based on how they lived their life on earth.[8]

Prevailing secular standards and even religious traditions are sometimes the biggest obstacle to preparing correctly for spirit world. Learning concepts, views and ideas about life after death that are not correct could lead to more difficulty than one bargained for. In any case, there is little preparation for this final eventuality in schools, homes or even religious institutions. Young people are highly educated in every subject except the ones that holds the key to the entire meaning of life, and perhaps to our very survival.[9] The fact that there isn't public funding for postmortem survival is an incredible shortcoming of modern society. Much research is undergone every day for new innovations and breakthroughs in almost every academic field of study. Yet, comparatively speaking very few resources are devoted to metaphysical studies. Ironically, most new discoveries are inspired by the spirit world. Insights, inspirations and creative achievement are not made by us, but by another person standing directly behind and above us.[10] The earth world has the spirit world to thank for all the major scientific discoveries that have been made throughout the centuries.[11]

The question still remains: What happens after we die? People that deal with death on a daily basis—ministers, police and emergency room doctors—don't necessarily agree on what takes place at death. It is a very humbling experience to be in that situation and not know what to think or feel. Sorry to say, religions have quite a few contrasting theories about the afterlife that complicate the matter even more.

The ancient Greeks used crystal gazing or scrying to create an environment where they communicate directly with their departed love ones without the help of a medium. In recent times, Dr. Raymond Moody has produced a chamber of off-kiltered mirrors called psychomanteums for people seeking reunion with their departed loved ones. By revitalizing this lost art of mirror gazing in the twilight hours, dead relatives come out and sit with their live family members and have conversation.[12]

Though these events seem bizarre, soon they may be just as natural as the physical reality around us.

Nevertheless, unbelievable accounts of anomalous experiences have been increasing over the last 150 years. While science and materialism have grown, there has been a parallel growth in the age of spiritualism since the mid-1800's. Since the nineteenth century, the Ouija board was used to make talking with the dead as natural as dinnertime conversation.[13] There has been an explosion of spiritual communication through mediums from the birth of Spiritualism with the Fox sisters to the more recent transcommunication coming from spirit world machines. There has always been a small but significant minority that has pursued the paranormal. Research on postmortem survival is not well-known but continues on a regular basis. Thus far, positive proof of life after death has been steadily forthcoming. Still, many men and women with sterling scientific and religious backgrounds are reluctant to speak out publicly of their paranormal experiences. Despite the fact that the majority of people have after death communication with loved ones by and large they never talk about them with others.[14] Sooner or later, sounds, voices or something out of the ordinary take place to cause them to ask: what was that and how did it happen? Hunches, intuitions and sixth sense premonitions are very hard to explain. Some people continue to just block it out. But by emptying oneself and connecting with a higher source, man can generate a greater capacity for knowledge. Emotional intelligence, of which gut feelings are a component, enables a different kind of knowing.[15] An entirely new world is opening up as man's spiritual senses are being restored.

The best place to study the afterlife is with death itself and what it might be like to die. Medieval man expected to see heavenly lights and talk to dead relatives as his vital signs failed.[16] Most of this evidence comes from near death experiences (NDEs). The tracking through polling of near death experiences shows millions of people worldwide continue to have out of the body (OBE) experiences. Not only have out of body experiences been reported throughout history, but on average one in five people will have an OBE at some point in his or her life.[17] The NDE also points to a verifiable existence of a vast spirit world. People who have experienced a NDE are left with no doubt that consciousness survives bodily death.[18] Out of the body experiences from dreaming in sleep have similar characteristics as near death experiences. The vividness of dreams and NDEs are so close to reality that they are sometimes difficult to distinguish between the two. The evidence points to an overlap between near death experiences and dreams, because they share the same limbic landscape.[19] Yet, no matter what the evidence, modern society's version of reality cannot accept the phenomenon of consciousness continuing after death. In other words, there is still a collective reluctance to embrace the reality of the spirit world.

SPIRIT WORLD

The invisible world, like the visible world, is a world of reality. Man desires to live forever because he has within himself a spirit man, which has an eternal nature.[20] Just as man can see, hear, touch, taste and smell the material world, he can see, hear, touch, taste and smell in the spiritual world. It is actually felt and perceived through the five spiritual senses.[21] The soul is made of energy that can be transformed but never destroyed. Once released from its physical body, the soul is free to travel to the spirit world, liberated from the rules and regulations of time and space that govern life on earth. When a human being's earthly life ends, he continues to the spirit world, but to different destinations according to his life on earth. When people on earth say they have seen someone who has moved on to the spirit world, they usually remark that the person looks younger and better than they ever did on the earth. We will live automatically on whatever vibrational level we deserve to be on, based on the quality of life we have lived while in the physical body.[22]

There is a general lack of knowledge that people on earth have about the afterlife. Ignorance about the afterlife can cause the dead unnecessary difficulty in making their transitions and adjusting to the afterlife.[23] When they cross over, they do not know what to expect. In so many cases it has to be explained to the newly awakened soul that he has died and is alive.[24] A large number of spirits experience a period of confusion when they first crossover after death. Virtually all the people who arrive there are astonished as they come to find that they are still alive. As a matter of fact, they are even more alive than when they were on the earth.

The experience of death is so subtle and painless most people don't realize what has happened to them. Since no one has a clear idea of what awaits them, many things seem strange. The manner, expectations, belief and mood at the time of death affects the soul's capability to make the switch to the afterlife. Rich or poor, well-educated or not, many share this baffling experience of not knowing where they are or how they got there. Swedenborg spoke of how many of those who move into the spirit world are unaware they no longer have a physical body and are now dead.[25] The fact they are still aware means, in their world-view, that they must be alive—nothing else is possible.[26] Spirits that believed that nothing exists after death are seriously confused and may refuse to accept their true condition for quite some time. To find oneself suddenly transformed into a permanent inhabitant of the spirit world is, at first, an overwhelming experience.[27]

There are almost an unlimited number of surprises that shock and overwhelm each person who enters the spirit world. Ignorance about what to expect in the afterlife is probably the biggest source of anguish and frustration for the newly departed. The feelings, thoughts and connections are the same as before death so preconceived notions and expectations complicate the transformation. By and large, the percentage of people who come to the spirit world with any knowledge of their new life and the spirit world is very low. Many feel like they are just dreaming and they keep waiting for something to happen that would break the dream into returning earthly consciousness.

Modern day haunting investigators often discover that a number of spirits have not figured out what has happened to them. It can be hard for those in spirit to realize they are dead because they continue to feel very much alive and seem to have a body. Those who do not believe in the afterlife may have an especially hard time understanding what happened. A spirit's personality is unaffected by death. They can see, hear, talk and touch and nothing at all seems to have change. Yet they have to find a new way to perceive and interact with the realm they now find themselves. The first step is for them to realize they are dead.[28] Understanding and accepting that they are truly dead may make it easier for them to separate from their physical body and be the first step toward the soul's integration and advancement in the spirit realm.[29]

The old saying, "You can't take it with you" is not true. All that is in man survives and is taken with him into the spirit world. The character and qualities of the spirit man are formed during the earthly life.[30] One of the great facts of spirit world is that souls are exactly the same after passing into spirit life as they were the instant before. After physical death, the same habits, perceptions and consciousness stay with each person. Communicators to the spirit world often refer to the departing soul as a kind of spiritual double of the physical body: one that is in appearance, an exact counterpart of the physical shape. Your astral body is a complete mirror of your physical body: it has a heart, liver, arms, legs a face, etc…but since it operates at a higher frequency, most people are unaware of it.[31]

The physical and spiritual bodies are bound together by many little threads, by two silver cords.[32] When someone dies, these threads and cords are gradually broken or severed. As the physical body dissolves, the spirit body adjusts to the new landscape. The newly departed have not lost their consciousness and remain fully aware of the feelings of those they left behind. So many souls of the earth are shocked to be told that the spirit world is a solid world, a substantial world, with real live people in it. Life as they had known it, no longer exists. To find out that the physical world is far from the only one they will inhabit leaves most people speechless. There is a certain similarity, a correspondence between the appearances of nature and the appearances on the celestial plane. Flowers are there, but these are shapes unknown to you, exquisite in color, radiant with light.[33] In effect, the physical world is just a shadow of the spirit world. Yet they simply cannot grasp the concrete existence of all the wonders and beauties and marvels that they see around them.[34] They are even more incredulous when they find out what brilliant prospects await them.

In previous times, people thought and experienced themselves as spirits inhabiting bodies. Virtually all of the world's shamanic traditions contain descriptions of the vast, extra dimensional realm, replete with references to the life review, higher spiritual beings who teach and guide, food conjured up out of thought and indescribably beautiful meadows, forests and mountains.[35] Modern man does not share this extrasensory outlook on life. When the present day scientific culture proclaims that the body is all there is and that the inner person doesn't exist, an instinctive conflict is felt. Today's society suppresses any thoughts or mention of death devaluing the mystical whereas tribal peoples still have day to day contact with the psychic nature of reality.[36] For the vast majority of peoples over the vast majority of history, the human being was understood to be at least a twofold creature: one that possessed a physical body visible to all and also invisible spiritual body: one that contained the thoughts and emotions that each of us feels.[37] In the present day, there is little concern for the soul as nearly everyone is concerned about their bodily needs. On earth you are on a treadmill and live with exhaustion, but there is no necessity to live like that in the world of Paradise.[38]

Until now people on the earth have not fully understood the concept of an enduring spiritual life. They think that only life on earth is important.[39] The spirit world is divided into many different realms or spheres. Those departing souls who arrive on the lowest of the astral planes find that they lack physical bodies and are bewildered by the almost total darkness that seems to surround them.[40] Those in the higher realms discover a completely different spirit world, where nothing is lacking. There with little effort anything can be gained and accomplished.

Most spirits are very hard on themselves for their mistakes forgetting the good they've done. The self-evaluation following death can be excruciating. Dealing with any disgraceful actions is a complicated issue. Everyone has to look back on their life on earth in order to better understand it and figure out how it could be improved. The life review is one of the most universal stages of passing over into the spirit world. Self-judgment is an essential step in the process of spiritual growth. The destination of the spirit man is decided by the spirit man himself, not by God.[41] Depending on whether bad or good is reflected back, it can be traumatic or uplifting. Everything is revealed. This can be embarrassing and discomforting at first. And while souls may grow accustomed to the fact that others see their shortcomings, their own awareness of these failures can be heartbreaking.[42] Sometimes re-experiencing the full details is an agonizing experience that brings more remorse than the worse judgment. Not only the memory but all the hurt that was caused is felt; the heartbreak of selfishness is perceived with no rationalizations. Any pain meant for others is experienced vicariously. Any hidden motivations and secret reasons for behavior are revealed. After the self-reflection from reviewing their life on earth, a close next step is a kind of self-judgment. Masters or great teachers make these intentions visible, and it is revealed as if watching a huge movie screen. It is intense method, demanding everyone look at themselves with unprotected eyes. As a result we look at ourselves afresh as naked souls, stained and bruised with the results of our selfish intentions and motivations that we know to be so deeply human.[43] Attitude and motivation adjustments are the focal points of seeing the results of their actions. There are no halls of judgment and God doesn't judge, instead each soul must review and judge its own life.[44] Most sources suggest that the motive or intent determines how the words and deeds are viewed. Any subsequent self-reprimand and regret is the worse form of punishment. Besides self-reflection, the spirit has to face quite a few other challenges in their new life on the other side. At first it is hard to recognize what their new state has gained them, given what they have lost.[45] Besides missing their usual habits, family and environment, their lack of knowledge or doubts can cause considerable problems. Adjusting to the fact that they can't interact or accomplish things the way they use to can lead to intense frustration. Having a new consciousness leads to a course of denial, anger, regret and eventual acceptance.

Without the right send off, spirits grieve as do their family and friends on earth. Many mediums have reported that wishing for the soul of a dearly departed to return is the worst thing you can do to someone who has died. In some cases, it is the grief of the living, felt with painful clarity by the dead, that hampers their transition.[46] When the living are inconsolable, it can make their loved ones in the spirit world even more sad because they are unable to do anything about it. The fact that their families on earth are still ignorant of this leads to even more anguish. They have a need to adjust to their new state but remain torn by the need to comfort those left behind. It is only when the reality of spirit world sinks in that natural development takes place. Eventually the spirits learn how to change their rate of vibration to be seen or heard by the living. Regardless of the type of transition to spirit world, the will to communicate with love ones continues in many unseen ways.

NEAR DEATH EXPERIENCE

As modern medical techniques for resuscitation advance, more near death experiences (NDEs) are being reported every year. In 1975, Dr. Raymond Moody Jr. wrote *Life After Life*, which chronicled ground breaking accounts of the phenomena of life after death. Moody believed that the profound and positive identity changes individuals undergo are the most compelling evidence that NDEs are actually journeys into some spiritual level of reality.[47] Dying patients continue to have a conscious awareness of their environment after being pronounced clinically dead. Not only do they make an unexpected comeback, but they have experiences outside this world that alters their lives. Most are greeted by loved ones who had died before them, or by a religious figure that coincided with their own religious beliefs. Ultimately, they are asked the question: "Are you prepared to die?" or "What have you done with your life?" The point of these questions causes them to think about their lives, to draw them out. Eventually the person who dies sees a panoramic review of his life, as if it was videotaped. The pictures progress through their whole life from the beginning to the present. Even the emotions and feeling associated with the images are re-experienced.

All this takes place in an instant of earthly time. This instructive effort seems to stress the importance of loving and not hurting others. Almost everyone interviewed by Moody wanted to stay in their new disembodied existence but they felt an obligation to come back to finish their responsibility or some important task left undone on the earth. Upon returning from their experience, they had no doubt as to its reality but did not feel comfortable telling just anyone about it.

There is great similarity across cultures and belief systems, arguing there is something "real" about NDEs.[48] Millions worldwide have had NDEs and although no two are identical, there is a familiar pattern of supernatural events. All NDEs elements appearing in Western NDEs are present in non-Western NDEs.[49] These similarities suggest that leaving the body is a simple, natural development that enables the spirit to move on to new realities. The level of consciousness during NDEs is usually much greater than what they experienced during their everyday life. Some of the experiences in a NDE include:

- Maintaining a similar body of a different kind
- Heightened senses, accompanied by a unique calmness
- Intense and generally positive emotions or feelings
- Passing into or through a tunnel
- Encountering a mystical or brilliant light
- Encountering other beings, often deceased relatives
- A sense of shift in time and space
- Having a life review

- Visiting different realms
- Learning special knowledge
- Encountering a boundary or barrier with reluctance to go back
- A return to the body, either voluntary or involuntary
- Experiencing intense feelings of joy, love and peace
- Personality transformation

For the most part, people who have a near death experience are generally convinced that after death a wonderful afterlife awaits them. The sensation of being freed of this earthly body was wonderful beyond description.[50] Even atheists are somewhat embarrassed by encountering a being of light who seems God like. The results are transformative, including unexpected healings of people with very serious illnesses. Many cannot find adequate words to describe these episodes. People that have a NDE have a decreased death anxiety and a greater zest for living than the normal population.[51] Through personally experiencing the afterlife, they are convinced that death is not the end but rather a transition to the next world. As a result, they have a greatly reduced fear of death. In fact, they enjoy sharing their experiences to help others who are grieving, feeling hopeless or doubt an afterlife. A typical NDE testimony may sound something like this:

I found myself floating up toward the ceiling. I could see everyone around the bed very plainly, even my own body. I thought how odd it was that they were upset about my body. I was fine and I wanted them to know that, but there seemed to be no way to let them know. It was as though there were a veil or a screen between me and the others in the room.

I became aware of an opening, if I can call it that. It appeared to be elongated and dark, and I began to zoom through it. I was puzzled yet exhilarated. I came out of this tunnel into a realm of soft, brilliant love and light. The love was everywhere. It surrounded me and seemed to soak through into my very being. At some point I was shown, or saw, the events of my life. They were in a kind of vast panorama. All of this is really just indescribable. People I knew who had died were there with me in the light. They were happy, beaming. I didn't want to go back, but I was told that I had to by a man in light. I was being told that I had not completed what I had to do in life. I came back into my body with a sudden lurch.

Remarkably, when someone leaves their physical body in a NDE, there is a total absence of panic, fear or anxiety. They are usually aware of the environment in which the accident or death occurs. This may be in the hospital after a coronary attack or at the scene of a tragic accident. They observe the people who work with the resuscitation team, or the people who work in a rescue attempt to extricate a mutilated and hurt body from a car wreck. They watch this at a distance of a few feet, in a rather detached state of mind. At this moment of observation of the scene of death they observe people's conversation, their behavior, their clothes, and their thoughts without having any negative feelings about the whole occurrence. Even totally blind people that have NDEs are able to immediately have full and clear vision. They are able to comprehend minute details of shape, color and designs that they never could see before. More amazingly, their observation not only included a multi-dimensionally 360 degree vision but they were able to focus as close or as far away as needed.

Most NDEs are peaceful and loving, but some are disturbing. If truth be told, people with negative experiences either repress them or are embarrassed to report them. Many resolve to remain silent for fear others would consider them mentally unstable. Some are able to share their stories with family and close friends. Afterwards, there is a heightened sense of intuition with a more profound approach toward life. Everything is known for what it is and for how it affects the inner self. They realize the things they previously thought were important were actually not in the grand scheme of things. There was more to life than just their daily schedule. A whole new world has opened to them, especially their attitude toward death. Without exception, no one was afraid of death anymore because they knew they were alive "somewhere else."

After an experience on the other side, a person no longer entertains any doubts about his survival of bodily death. It is no longer a vague concept or an abstract possibility—it is a fact of their own experience. They return not only firmly convinced of the immortality of the human soul, but also with a deep and abiding sense that the universe is compassionate and intelligent, and this loving presence is always with them.[52] A true humbling takes place as the whole progression of life become visible. Many describe the event like a rerun of a play or film or like watching it on the screen. Many NDErs say the life review was the greatest catalyst for change after they returned to earth. There is no way to build a façade or mask one's problems. What was sown on earth is reaped in the spirit world. The only judgment that takes place is self-judgment and arises out of the NDErs own feelings of guilt and repentance.[53]

The life review clearly indicates that NDErs retain their memories for visual images, emotions and their own actions and behavior. A life review allows NDErs to relive their own lives, mistakes and all. During this instantaneous and panoramic remembrance NDErs re-experience all the emotions, the joys and sorrows of every part of their life. More than that, they feel all of the emotions of the people whom they have interacted as well.[54] Some experiences are frightening possibly as retribution for the bad things that had been done. During the process they witness the good and the bad, the cause and effect of their choices. They not only relived their own emotions but also others' reactions to their earthly actions. It seemed "right" to experience the pain that one has caused and know it for what it is.[55] It gives them a chance to evaluate themselves on their life performance to that point. Many NDE researchers have noted that one of the life's review main lessons is that knowledge and love are two elements that they take with them.

As a result, people who have NDEs become more loving in their interactions and they especially value positive and empathic relations. NDEs trigger lifestyle changes, more feelings of love and joy, greater compassion and a renewal or deepening of spiritual beliefs.[56] Many of their values and understandings are re-evaluated. They are made more aware of the needs of others and are willing to reach out to them. In brief, they have had a transformational change which leads to a richer, more fulfilling life. Those individuals who were afraid of death beforehand may no longer be so, but may even look forward to it. After the review is done, the memories are discarded once the lessons of life are learned.[57] As a result, NDErs have increased confidence, a stronger sense of spirituality, a reduced interest in material gain or status and a greater appreciation of life. Other after effects include: a belief in the sacredness of life, a sense of God's presence and an awareness of the meaning and purpose of life. It has been said by many who have had near-death experiences that God's presence is felt everywhere in the spirit world.[58]

Researchers have discovered that NDErs are almost always profoundly changed by their journey to the beyond. Their previous view of the afterlife is abandoned for one of cooperative development towards an ultimate end of self-realization. They become happier, more optimistic, more easygoing and less concerned with material possessions.[59] Above and beyond documented miraculous healings, many have "awakened" to new found intelligence. Increased memory, knowledge and an elevated intuition are just some of the excellent after effects. There is a new confidence that all of life's problems can be solved.

What's more a new ability of wholeness is attained. For amputees, they mentally have their legs again. If they were deaf mutes, they feel they can hear and talk even though it is medically impossible. For someone born blind, there is the renewed hope of gaining clear and detailed visual ability. Even someone with multiple sclerosis in a wheelchair is able to image singing and dancing again. People who have had a near-death experience are never the same.[60] Some even acquired psychic ability.

The near death experience tells us that we all have an inner voice, if only we would listen to it, that death is not to be feared and that life is to be lived to the fullest.[61] In NDEs, a kind of universal knowledge is imparted and wondrous glimpses of heaven are experienced. According to people who have visited the astral realm during the out of body or near death experiences, there are landscapes, oceans, flora, fauna, and even buildings in this other world, the same as in the physical world because they have been created by the minds of the beings who inhabit it and who previously lived on earth.[62] Knowledge of the important things in life comes into focus and even previously suicidal people realize that life has a purpose. Altogether, the NDE experience may be the closest experience of understanding the transition of death into the spirit world.

The Near Death Experience Research Foundation has over 2500 full-text published NDE accounts, much of it is subjective based on personal experiences. The mass of evidence for these after death experiences has stood up to the strictest examination. The picture of reality reported by NDErs is remarkably self-consistent and is collaborated by the testimony of many of the world's most talented mystics as well.[63] NDE researchers estimate that between 43 and 60 percent of the people who come close to death will have a near death experience. Most of the people experience the positive emotions of peace, joy, happiness and love. However, there are small percentages that have difficult or dark experiences. Either way, they all know there is always going to be a tomorrow.

ANGELS

Jewish, Christian and Islamic traditions believe that angels are assigned to protect and care for each person. These benevolent spirits dispense blessings to the human world and protect people from harm.[64] Most people are aware of their presence yet stories about angels have always inspired man. Angels act as mediators or go betweens for God and humankind, often going back between heaven and earth.[65] One thing is for sure, there is perpetual human fascination about angels. Many people have a great attraction for angels surrounding themselves with their artistic images. Angel expressions penetrate all aspects of human society. Churches, schools, businesses, investor organizations, sport teams, books, songs and many TV shows depict these spiritual benefactors as they demonstrate exceptional ability to protect and influence. Throughout history, angels have appeared in distinguishing works of art. Angel shaped beings appeared in ancient Mesopotamian and Greek art. Popular Christian images of angels later appeared in Byzantine and European paintings and sculpture. Nineteenth and twentieth century art and literature often mirrored angels for spiritual aspiration.[66]

Angels are said to have extraordinary power, and are often objects of worship. Evil forces are essentially helpless against them. Angels also perform many ecclesiastical, civil and domestic services.[67] Swedenborg understood the mission of angels was to protect people on earth from the influence of evil spirits. The garments worn by angels are immersed in light that makes the brightest lights on Earth seem like darkness.[68] Yet the reluctance to talk about angels contrasts powerfully with the awe from being in their presence. Many people have encountered them on the threshold of death. Angels are believed to escort souls to heaven but rarely reveal themselves until then. When we die, our spiritual senses open and we immediately realize that we are not alone—because our guardian angel is there.

The history of angels is intriguing. Angels have been used as God's instruments to guide humans along the right path—thus the name "guardian angels" became accepted. Their service to God is usually by delivering a particular thought, knowledge or counsel that is needed at a certain crisis point. There are countless stories written about angels providing protection and comfort for human beings. They console through trials and help souls find their way back to the state of awareness of their spiritual life. Angelic actions are not really miraculous because they are naturally within the bounds of their created nature. They are endowed with special qualities that enable God to use them to convey his love. They communicate by impressing upon our minds heavenly thoughts. Angels protect us when God wants us protected, by playing unseen but pivotal roles at key moments in our lives.

According to some religious tradition, angels can temporarily take on a form to enable ordinary persons to consciously see and hear them.[69] They are involved in everyone's life and they try to convey information if something needs to be known. Angels guide every important event in life and their mission is to help wherever there is a need. They are always close by, encouraging, consoling, warning, coaching, and leading man to achieve the purpose for which he was created—to think in concert with God and the universe. From the moment of birth until the moment of death, a personal angel is there to watch over and assist in the transition from the physical world to the spiritual world. These guardians function as guides or companions to every person as they travel up the tunnel on their journey to the light.[70]

When someone has a pure heart and is aligned with God's will, angels are obliged to help. Angels are caring and compassionate beings interested in only serving man and his Creator to the fullest of their abilities. Acknowledging and inviting their presence greatly helps them to assist in our lives.[71] Some general knowledge about angels may well include:

- Angels want nothing more than to help people, to teach them, to lead them into heaven. This is their highest joy.
- Angels have no notion or concept of location, time or space.
- The clothes they wear correspond to their mission and intelligence, the highest being the most radiant.
- There are an infinite number of angels, sent by God to give us joy and peace
- Angels have will, intellect, love, wisdom, memory, power, language, and form.

22

- Angels do everything for newly arrived spirits to spirit world, sharing freely about the realities of the next life.
- Angels are motivated by God's providence to secure the kingdom of heaven on earth

Angels have been part of the Divine plan since the beginning, so it seems that God wanted mankind to know about them and to feel free to ask them for protection. God created the angels as servants who were to assist in the creation of the universe, and in his dispensation for it.[72] Many people can scarcely believe that angels have the mission to minister to human beings as servants. Whether they're protecting us from harm, saving lives, or simply bringing messages of comfort and love, angels are truly God's mightiest link, most direct link between here and the spiritual world.[73] The angels are largely concerned with the health, well being, and advancement of man and the entire creation. An experience with an angel usually defies the known laws of nature which make it even more difficult to explain. Many people have had miraculous experiences that have saved, cured or comforted them when there was a dire emergency.

Angels often come to people in dreams. Survivors of near-death experiences often cite "beings of light" that they meet along their way. Angelic action is usually rep-resented as a movement of light so it is difficult to com-prehend. The wonder of how much God loves mankind through these 24/7 helpers humbles even the most un-bending non-believer. Ironically, the innocent acceptance of this fact by children enables them to be recipients of the wonders of heaven's spiritual messengers. Yet, angels can manifest to anyone, anywhere to demonstrate their power, wisdom and kindness.

We tend to be more open to angels as helpers than as bearers of God's truth.[74] Yet, many of the earliest stories about angels come from the Bible. In the Old Testament, Abraham, Jacob, Moses, Joshua, Elijah, Gideon and Daniel all received the benefits of angelic intervention. One of the most famous is the story describing Jacob's vision of angels ascending and descending a ladder that connected him with God. Angels conveyed to Abraham important words of blessing from God. In the New Testament, angels are recorded in several interactions surrounding Jesus' life and ministry. The angel Gabriel appeared to Zechariah to announce the birth of their son, John. Angel's heralded Mary conception of Jesus, told Joseph when to flee with his family to Egypt, appeared at Jesus' tomb, unchained Peter and led him out of prison. In later centuries, Muhammad was given instructions by the Archangel Gabriel to establish Islam and the Book of Mormon was revealed to Joseph Smith through the angel Moroni.

The most common story about angels is about individuals who are miraculously helped by someone whom they cannot locate to thank. There is good reason to believe that these strangers are angels. Throughout scripture angels do not linger or develop an ongoing relationship with people. Angels never seek credit for what they do, nor do they wait around to be thanked. They usually do their work and leave unnoticed so that all the glory will go to God. They can appear in any complexion, height, gender or ethnic character and can adapt to any situation, at any time, to fill almost any need.

Today, people worldwide are able to share their miraculous angelic experiences online. More and more people are learning about the daily help that is available from angels through books, articles, seminars and videos. More than a few television episodes and major movies have illustrated the interaction between humans and the angelic world. Yet considering they have been around since the beginning—not that much is known about these invisible creatures.

The hierarchies of angels most accepted in Christian tradition are nine choirs or levels of angels. *The Celestial Hierarchies*, written by Pseudo–Dionysius, maps out the heavens and ranks the angels. Thomas Aquinas also wrote about this account of the angels in his *Summa Theologica*. The nine choirs of heaven include:

1. Seraphim—the highest order of angels are the angels of love, pure light and fire. They are known for praising God while they guard his throne in heaven.

2. Cherubim—They represent knowledge and are the keepers of the divine records of the universe since the beginning of time, including human experience, animals and minerals.

3. Thrones—bridge the material and spiritual to carry out God's justice. They guard the throne of God.

4. Dominions—they regulate the activities of the other angels and keep the universe running smoothly.

5. Virtues—they are entrusted with the movement and operations of nature and play a role in inspiring works of art and scientific discoveries.

6.Powers—they preserve order and purify the universe from lower energies. Powers oversee conscience and history and are the angels of birth and death.

7. Principalities—They are guardians of entire nations. They are protectors of religion and work to insure God's will of peace.

8.Archangels—They look after the affairs of humankind, are guardians of heaven and oversee the angels

9.Angels—as servants perform many duties especially dealing with sending messages back between the spirit world and the physical world. They are assigned to each person at the time of birth. There are many types of guardian or guiding angels. Their missions include protection, comfort, mercy, peace, hope, virtue, love, grace, encouragement, instruction, truth, healing and happiness.

One thing's for sure, angels are an integral part of man's history and are here to stay.

HEAVEN

The Abrahamic religions of Christianity and Islam describe a very rewarding afterlife for those with good behavior. Mediums who have visited heaven say it's beautiful beyond description. For centuries, Christian ministers have echoed St. Paul when they tell their congregations that words cannot express the awesome spectacle of heaven.[75] Tibetan Buddhism recognizes the existence of 28 divine realms attained by those who have gained exceptional merit in their earthly lives.[76] In heaven, anything imaginable is possible and nothing is impossible. Most people can hardly believe that such a place exists let alone that they were born to live in it forever. In heaven:

- Clothes are incorruptible and do not wear out
- There is no disintegration, so there is no dust or dirt to clean
- Buildings, furniture and other things do not get worn out with age
- No one can get hurt as our spirit bodies are impervious to all injury
- Inhabitants enjoy a state of perfect health; there is no illness or disease
- The prime of life is the permanent age
- There are no handicaps or deformities

- All animals are harmless and gentle; having no fear and no enemies.
- Flowers, shrubs, trees and fruit are always in season
- Painting are alive, glowing with color and life
- Manuscripts of recorded history contain only true facts
- Music sounds are pure, clear and integrated with form and colors
- There is no need for food or sleep
- There are no physical problems, so no need for crutches or eyeglasses
- Language is no barrier as thoughts can be transmitted mentally
- There is no divisions due to race, nationality, religion or gender
- Transportation and communication are instantaneous
- Since there are no cars, there are no traffic jams, no lines, no obstacles
- The water and the air is astonishing clear and cannot be polluted
- No one works for a living, only for the sheer joy of doing something
- There are libraries of learning for music, science and art among others

Equally amazing is the absence of work in spirit world. No destructive forces can effect it. Many other things that are normal on earth do not exist there. For example, there is:

- No food industry as there is no need for food or drink
- No communication system as thoughts are transmitted instantaneously
- No transportation systems as travel is direct and immediate
- No manufacturing plants as things wanted can be willed
- No waste removal industry as everything is naturally recycled
- No utilities for power
- No banking system for money
- No businesses to acquire goods

What is life like in heaven? In heaven, beauty is without end. Every square inch of land and water is magnificently, eternally new.[77] The sky is a beautiful blue, the clouds are as fairy clouds, tinted with pink, purple, gold and white that float in the beautiful deep azure blue skies. There are no earthquakes, volcanoes or catastrophic weather patterns. There is no wind stronger than an occasional gentle breeze, no heat waves, and no cold fronts.[78] Rain, snow, sleet and hail are absent. The hills are covered with a deep green of grass on the astral plane. It has gorgeous trees, flowers, shady glades, rushing streams, towering mountains, sparkling lakes, charming little villages, large cities, vast oceans and plenty of animals. It is an unending vista of magnificent buildings built of precious stones set amid the most entrancing richness of color and grandeur of form. This is what was christened by NDErs as the Summerland.[79]

In heaven, everything looks beautiful, everything sounds wonderful and you feel content with everything around you. In heaven, beautiful green grass, mountains, lakes and prairies are everywhere. Birds sing, flowers bloom in profusion, and animals play happily together. The air is fresh and filled with fragrances like lilac. Bright light shines throughout, more beautiful than diamond and clear as crystal. The sun shines perpetually with equal intensity from all directions. Everything is so much more vivid and brilliant than it is on earth.[80] In all places one feels comfortable and refreshed. The air is filled with thoughts of love and happiness. It is a world filled with God's love. The essence of this love is to live for the sake of the whole, rather than to be served.[81] Unlike earthly life where happiness comes and goes, in heaven joy is felt continually. There is no anxiety or suffering. All the spirits have bright and peaceful expressions. There is no fighting, no jealousy and no animosity. They naturally care for each other without needing to say a word. In heaven, intuitive sensations become real. Everything has wavelengths that resonate with the mind like a tuning fork. Pure love, wisdom and harmony are the essences that encompass the ultimate reality of heaven.

This sphere of life is the true one because it is permanent.[82] There are no worries about what to eat, where to live and what to wear. The air you breathe in the spirit world is made of love.[83] Everyone can exercise independent, unlimited creativity without end. Everything you wish for will become reality.[84] The great majority can scarcely contemplate a state of greater beauty and happiness.[85] Earthly gardens at their best and finest are very poor by comparison to the breathtaking gardens that exude perfect coloring and heavenly perfumes.[86] In heaven, the environment abounds with many dazzling jewels. The light of heaven shines evenly and uninterruptedly, so nowhere are there dark places. Since there is no darkness people can carry on their activities of travel, amusement, study, work or entertainment as long as they want. It is a place of play and work where everyone is constantly growing by actively contributing. Unity and mutual agreement with others is natural and accepted. One never gets tired of experiencing new things or suffers any kind of fatigue. The work and growth achieved is profoundly fulfilling. The only distress one may feel is the realization that their earthly attitudes were mistaken. So much so, that when someone looks back on their life on earth, they are rather shocked by the quite ridiculous importance placed on some trivial incident.[87] Only to find out later why God allowed those terrible things to happen and how He found a way to use them to accomplish a greater good.

On earth, there is scarcely enough time to do what one wants to do. Since life in heaven is timeless, there are always opportunities to visit anyplace and to share ideas with anyone. Interacting with famous personalities is no problem. Any person can immediately appear if there is a feeling of true love. Even an ancestor from a different era can appear. These may include the most notable artists, musicians, athletes, explorers, political leaders, philosophers, military men, writers, scientists, reformers, saints and even God himself. In heaven, it is no problem to travel millions of miles in an instant. You can commute a tremendous distance in an instant.[88] However, if one desires to travel in open air cars or trains, they are immediately available to go anywhere. In heaven, anything can be attained or known instantly. Everything can be created through ideas.[89] There is instant availability of live entertainment. The most unusual requests can come about naturally. For example, someone can wear whatever clothes they want or eat whatever they like if that is their wish.

Spirits design their own personal heavens according to their desires. Heaven is never the same for any two people. Some live in mansions, some in high-rise apartments and some in country houses. Among the busiest, most treasured, and most prolific structures are the vast libraries, schools, and research centers.[90] In the spirit world, historical books report exactly what happened, not someone's opinion of what occurred.[91] These environments for study combine majestic surroundings with peacefulness and serenity. Concert halls filled to capacity offer nonstop appearances by the most brilliant performing artists and speakers humankind has ever known. Sporting activities and social gatherings abound in imposing environments. The most notable feature of these great cities is that they are brilliantly luminous.[92] The world's most prize possessions are nothing by comparison.

Principally, the kingdom of heaven is the place where people who have no individualism or self-centered thought gather and live.[93] The heart of love for the sake of others is the natural way of life. Because of the surrounding brightness, nothing is hidden even between people. Everything can be seen and known with the eyes and the mind. It is the place where the mind is always filled with peace and serenity, where difficulty, discomfort and hunger do not exist. A spirit person in heaven can know completely all of

God's creation process from the beginning. What's more, spirit people continue to evolve to higher levels and no one will be jealous.

Communication is by the heart, not by the lips. Heaven is the place where you find no difficulty to express or explain anything.[94] At the same instant a spirit person thinks, another spirit person can receive it, and it doesn't require words. The primary means of communication is telepathy. All five spiritual senses are precise, clear and active. From science to music to architecture, heaven is a joyful, absorbing place, full of exciting things to do. By all accounts it is an ideal futuristic world coupled with exquisite natural beauty.

Even more notable is that there is no status, power, titles or position based on education, wealth or social standing. Everyone is equally blessed and no one is superior to anyone else. It is the great leveler. Each person is created with their own unique potential that has a divine destiny. On earth, money, knowledge and power are necessary, but there is no need for them in the spirit world.[95] The divine spirit world has much to communicate to the earth. However, the earth must first put itself in responsible correlation to the spirit world. Most importantly, the people of earth must learn to not to turn to evil purposes that which was transmitted to it for good and peaceful purposes. It is for man himself to choose.[96]

According to conventional belief, there are three levels of heaven. Those who sincerely tried to live a life of goodness according to their conscience, including patriots, charitable and publicly minded people inhabit the lower realm of heaven. The next level of heaven is the dwelling place of all those good religious people who, through their devotion to God, unreserved dedicated themselves in love and service to others.[97] In the highest realms dwell those of advanced spirituality who have genuinely lived for the sake of humanity. These include the founders of the great religions and their dedicated followers. All of these realms embody the full awareness of God's divine love.

To restate, the lifestyle in this realm of spirit world is very different than the way things are on earth. There is no garbage, no dust, no traffic, no industrial waste, no heating or cooling, no bodily illness, no way to physically injure oneself or another, and no difficulty getting from one place to the other. There are no trucks, no appliances, no factories, no landfills, no laundries, no banks, no stock exchanges, no cemeteries, no felling of forests, no emergency rooms, no bomb factories and no lawyers. In this environment, telephones, radio or e-mailing have no significance because communication is instantaneous. In this realm you have plenty of energy without eating or sleeping.[98] There is an immense amount of teaching, counseling, building, gardening, craftsmanship and artistic expression. Music is the supreme art form, along with painting, dance and theater. There is an abundance of flowers everywhere. Libraries abound and books of knowledge, insight and wisdom are cherished. There are plenty of professions as different products, structures and cities have to be built. Work takes on a completely different value because there is no need to worry about money to earn a living. Everyone is filled only with true love and lives for the sake of others.[99]

In essence, earthly life and life in heaven are correspondingly dissimilar. People on earth live for their own sake, but people in heaven live for others. Value is based on the frequency of love, not money, power or education. Strength is in service not in external power. Fulfillment is based on experiencing God's love not self-centered love. On earth everyone has their own goals but in heaven everyone has a similar goal is to advance toward perfection and perpetual happiness.[100] Which explains why everyone naturally wants to go to heaven.

HELL

The attractiveness of heaven is nearly matched by the notoriety of hell. Since the earliest recorded history, suffering in the afterlife has been seen as consequences for wrongdoing in the physical life. Eastern and Western traditions are alike in that there is no escaping retribution for sinful actions. Even the ancient Greeks, with their misty poetic descriptions of Hades, believed that a sub-Hades level existed for the souls of the really wicked, who faced punishments of ingenious nastiness appropriate to their earthly misdeeds.[101] Images of hell are found throughout history especially from the fourth to the fourteenth century in religious literature. Even today, hell continues to be a "hot" topic because of man's fascination with this reprehensible destination in the afterlife.

The history of hell has different versions including the Mesopotamian, the Babylonians, the Egyptians, the Greeks, the Hebrews and the Christians. Also called the Land of the Dead, the Underworld, the Lower World, Sheol and Hades, hell has been part of man's image of the afterlife since the beginning of recorded history. The subject of hell brings up a huge amount of stress and fear. It is an inconvenient truth that most people cannot deal with. If truth be told, many people do not believe that hell exists.[102] The truth about the existence of hell has troubled thinkers for a long time.

The idea of eternal torment causes fearful discomfort even in the most dull-witted mind. It is a lonely, dark reality that shapes some people's future more than they care to admit.

Despite guideposts and warnings, many are not convinced that such a prison with little chance of escape exists. Many religions don't talk about it and many pastors don't want to offend people by continuing to tell them that this is the place to avoid. The ill-fated fact is that people make the choices to go to hell everyday if they drift and live sinful lives. Sobering accounts and testimonies of such a place are in different scriptures with descriptions of torment mentioned some 150 times in the Bible. Remote viewers who have seen many different parts of the next world have seen the huge mass of ex-physical humans, writhing and struggling in an endless attempt to have sex with one another.[103] The odors, the strength of the demons, the loudness of the screams, the dryness, and the loneliness felt were a thousand times worse than what would be possible on the earth's surface...I was extremely nauseous from the terrible, foul stench coming from those creatures...purpose was nonexistent...it was a reality filled with an endless eternity of pain, loss, loneliness and doom—a most miserable existence.[104]

Descriptions of hell fluctuate, but fundamentally it is the opposite of heaven. The Christian doctrine of hell is the most unmistakable, with a great escape possible only through belief in Jesus Christ. Those in hell are people who tried to justify their sins and are unrepentant. The sign at the gate of hell reads, "Abandon Hope All Ye Who Enter Here" according to Dante Alighieri. His *Divine Comedy* has always fascinated readers for its vivid descriptions of the infrastructure and inhabitants of the afterlife's different realms. In the year 1300AD, Dante travels through the different sections of the spirit world which included the Paradiso, the Purgatorio and the Inferno. People who sinned but prayed for forgiveness before their deaths are found not in hell but in purgatory where they toil to be free of their sins. But hell is like a gigantic funnel that leads to the very center of the earth. According to legend used by Dante, a huge, gigantic hole in the Earth was made when God threw Satan and his band of rebels out of heaven with such force that they created a giant hole in the earth. In the Inferno, he travels through the nine circles of hell. He meets the spirit of Virgil who takes him through the gates of hell where he encounters the suffering of all the damned at different levels depending on their sins. The circles are concentric representing a gradual increase in wickedness, and culminating at the centre of the earth, where Satan is held in bondage. Each circle's sinners are punished in a fashion fitting their crimes: sinners are afflicted by the chief sin they committed. The sights and sounds of the unending pain and cries frighten Dante to faint more than once. The cruelty of naked men pursued and torn to pieces by subhuman beasts is unimaginable. His descriptions of hell's darkness along with the moaning and shrieking of sinners would make anyone shudder with terror.

The lower a person travels in hell, the more grotesque it becomes. In short, it is absolute, retributive torment. Earthly horror, anguish and suffering pale in comparison to what happens in hell. Flaming deserts, a rain of fire, giant snakes, wasps and violent storms are part of the visions of hell. The intricate detail of tortures that have no limits or termination shocks even the most cynical skeptic. The thought of being trapped in such an unpleasant place would make anyone avoid a sinful life.

Swedenborg affirms that, according to the law of cosmic balance, there are three fundamental hells that correspond to the three levels of heaven—an outermost hell, which is least hellish, an intermediate hell, and an inmost hell which is the absolutely miserable dwelling place of the most cruel, depraved spirits of all.[105] According to Swedenborg, the malevolence that emanates from hell is a constant effort to destroy everything good and true. On the first level reside thieves, adulterers, drunks and misers. Depending on the severity of their crimes, the second and third levels are reserved for those who have committed rape, murder and torture. This realm of hell is described as a cold and menacing land, the roads—rough and precipitous, with a repugnant, evil smelling slime covering the surfaces everywhere. With poisonous vapors coming out of the ground, human beings crawl like foul beasts with little or no clothing. There is deep, impenetrable darkness, the ground is hard and barren, very few dwellings and not a soul to be seen anywhere.[106] Gloomy, dark and cold is the only way to describe it.[107] In this miserable region are earth's true sociopaths, remorseless and amoral, valuing no life but their own. They see the rest of humanity as a vast sea of pawns to be played with, used, manipulated and in some form or another—destroyed.[108] Hell is populated by people who have led predominately selfish lives, either actively or passively, and who have habitually sought to misuse or sacrifice other people in order to benefit themselves.[109] There are millions of spirits there who created their own hell by the way they sacrifice others for themselves. The inhabitants look sub-human with an outward appearance of the most hideous and repulsive malformations. Their faces are barely human – distorted and deformed. One has to wonder what earthly misdeeds caused this awful state of degeneration.

Some NDErs have experienced what is called Shad-owland or the realm of the unprogressed. Everything is dark and forbidding, and a dull laden fog pervades the air at all times. There are no flowers, no dwellings and every-where seems bleak and barren. The ground is hard and barren with no grass. The temperature is chilly, the sur-roundings foreboding and the sounds menacing. The in-habitants are the scum of the earth and have passed their lives in vice and crime. It has a large population that lives in discord and misery. The endless, confining state of dark, de-pressing misery intimidates the inhabitants. The residents of these realms of darkness have, by their lives on earth, condemned themselves to the state they find themselves in. The seeds of hideousness sown upon the earth-plane will inevitably lead to the reaping of a harvest of hideous-ness in the spirit world.[110] The ugliness of mind and deed can produce nothing but ugliness. There is no hope or joy because everyone is fearful, angry or annoyed. Centuries of humanity's hatred, greed, lust, jealousy and other unvirtu-ous desires litter the lowest realms of the spirit world. In hell, there is no beautiful life to be seen especially because of the bad odor and darkness. Here in the dark lands all is bleak and desolate.[111]

In some hells, there are what look like the ruins of houses and cities, where hellish spirits live and hide. There are many different hells, each one populated by people with a specific energy pattern like thieves, murderers, rapists, etc.[112] There are brothels, foul to look at and full of all kinds of filth and excrement. There are hellish spirits in homes filled with constant quarrels, hostility and violent beatings. The buildings appear dark, stained with great splashes of blood and covered with slimy fungus growth.[113] There are also dark forests where hellish spirits roam like wild beasts. Their bodies presented the outward appearance of the most hideous and repulsive malformations and distortions, the absolute reflection of their evil minds.[114]

It is a dark, dismal, uninviting place filled with countless numbers of souls who are lost and wandering about in great distress.[115] In hell, everyone feels uncomfortable, always uneasy and restless. There you endure hunger taking others possessions and eating by stealth.[116] It is truly a miserable existence. Anyone who has experienced the pangs of intense loneliness, remorse, shame or guilt recognizes that such states of mind are excruciatingly painful. On earth there are methods like sleep, drugs and alcohol to forget, rationalize and lose oneself. Yet in the spirit world there is no respite from the unpleasant feelings, the loneliness, the foul odors and the darkness that torture the soul continually. All are weighed down by the evil deeds of their earthly lives.

The malice of hellish spirits are too gruesome to convey. Tibetan Buddhism holds that at least 18 hells exist, including cold hells of shivering wretchedness and hot hells of barbequed unpleasantness for all those whose store of bad karma outweighs their good.[117] One Buddhist version of hell offers an equally horrible possibility: the wardens of hell will drive red-hot iron stakes through the victim's hands, feet and chest to prevent him from struggling. Then, using the sharp razors, they will shave off his flesh, head downwards.[118] In the Sufi vision of hell, sinners will roast in a burning fire, drink water from a boiling spring, are bitten by scorpions as large as mules and by serpents as big as camels.[119] The bestialities, barbarities, cruelties and grossness of hell are beyond belief. You could never die, that was the awful curse of the thing, and it was no use trying to kill yourself or get others to kill you, there was no such escape from suffering.[120] Hell is the absolute condition of karmic suffering.[121]

If you descend further into the lower regions, you come to the regions of hell that are even more suffocating, dark and scary. They smell horribly, worse than the smell of rotten meat or fish. Deformed figures appear, biting each other, yelling at each other in hate-filled voices. Some hells are places of isolation, others are cities of shared horrors, presided over by tyrannical rulers with very nasty temperaments, and stronger wills than their subjects.[122] Swedenborg observed that the only way to control the violent rages of people in hells is through fear of punishment. It is like a real unthinkable nightmare. People on earth do not realize how frightening the regions of hell really are.[123] The lower level is full of negative energy by souls who have committed a range of crimes but who refuse to accept their own death. In hell, the inhabitants cry out in torment and a heavy blackness looms over everything.

While heaven is a world of light, hell is a world of chaotic darkness where evil people exist together. There is no kindness, no friendship and no love.[124] Souls there are in great torment as a result of their own actions. They arrive there by their own hand.[125] People suffer from continual pangs of conscious and their lives are filled with distrust and anxiety. It is a miserable existence because everything desired is unable to be attained. Nothing is attainable because everything is locked away. Hell is a place where things don't make sense and the lack of order is as painful and horrific to experience as all the other things that go on there.[126] Hell is like a warehouse in which evil people deal with and sort out their problems. The environment in hell is dark where like a prison, there is no freedom. There is nothing to eat or to wear.[127]

Hell is a state of affairs where an ounce of prevention is worth a pound of cure. Here souls suffer indescribable pain to make atonement for evil deeds carried out on the earth. Each sinner is subjected to a punishment that is the exact opposite of their sin. For example, the punishment of thieves is that their hands, which they used to steal, are cut off. Someone that was trying to always get ahead of others finds themselves continuously crawling out of a quicksand pit. Those that spoke ill of others, find they cannot speak. There are desert areas where everything is barren and sandy where those craftier than others are exiled. Those who live for themselves carrying false pride, are many whom are bound in chains upside down.[128] Those who succeeded in earthly life by slandering and plotting against others will be turned upside down in the spirit world.[129] The feelings of being like a trapped animal come from never being able to forget the injustice perpetrated and given to another. All the impure desires of the lives of men on earth are collected in a great swamp of foulness where spirits wallow.[130] When the spirit body is starved or neglected, spiritual blindness, deafness and dumbness result.[131]

The link between deed and retribution is not severed by death. Problems of alcoholism, drug abuse and other addictions carry over into the spirit world. Every person reaps the fruits of their actions. This is the reason that life in the physical world, not knowing God, can easily become preparation for hell.[132] In addition, those who do not feel remorse, or who are unable or unwilling to learn what they have been taught, may remain in the lower astral level for many years, perhaps even centuries. No one has to be stuck but can move to higher levels as soon as they are ready, regardless of their situation or manner of their passing. The problem is that most spirits in darkness are too embarrassed to even acknowledge their mistakes or the help offered to them. Fortunately, everybody knows someone, so it almost always the case that someone will help them. Every spirit hates the lower levels of the spirit world and for that reason great organizations exist to help others to rise out of their hell and into the light. They are helped by others who are more advanced and who instruct them in the ways that exist to progress out of their deplorable condition. Sooner or later an encounter will occur with one of the compassionate beings who willingly give their time to lead tormented souls to a place of rest and enlightenment.[133] Even those souls who wind up in the lower plane need not remain stuck, but may escape with the help of higher beings. The golden opportunity of spiritual recovery is always ready and waiting. One has to but show an earnest desire to move one fraction of an inch towards the realms of light that are above him, and he will find unknown friends who him towards the heritage which is his due.[134] Modern day channelers recognize that spirit helpers exist whose function is to help lost souls move forward spiritually to a better place of existence.

For those who are heedless and do not prepare, death comes suddenly, fearfully and leaving them with regret.[135] The theme of divine retribution against evil permeates the Old Testament texts.[136] There are many ethical questions of hell's justice that are still subjects of numerous debates. Why would a God of love allow such evil and suffering to exist? Is hell meant to be a compensative justice or is it God's motivation to help people repent? How could God be compassionate, merciful and forgiving on one hand, yet relentlessly vengeful on the other? Is justice served by retribution or mercy? These questions regarding the beginning and end to hell have troubled theological thinkers for quite some time.

All mankind is destined to restore their lost position and status as lords of creation once the necessary conditions to reverse any wrongs are set up.[137] According to the law of compensation, also called the law of indemnity, when man fulfills his responsibility to reverse what was lost through his criminal actions, he can raise himself back to his original position. The law of compensation awakens the soul to the iniquities it premeditated and causes it to toil to pay it out. If one in hell can begin to pray to God, asking for his Divine Love, spiritual progress is accelerated.[138] Anyone can escape the torments of hell if they call out in repentance and seek for assistance. The damaged soul returns to heaven by way of Divine Love.

MEDIUMS

Mediumship dates back to early human history, when shamans healed sicknesses, predicted future events and communicated with the spirit world. For at least 2,500 years and across virtually all countries and cultures one can find stories of messages received from spirits who exist on another plane of reality. Although seemingly new, they are as old as recorded time. Mediums and channeling appear to have been part, even at the root, of most of the world's religions.[139]

Extraordinary claims of psychic phenomenon, paranormal events, telepathy, clairvoyance, channeling, astral travel and spiritual communication appear to contradict today's scientific methodology. Yet, psychic phenomenon has been notably increasing for over a hundred and fifty years. An explosive growth in paranormal activity began in the late 1840's in a modest farmhouse in Hydesville, near Rochester in upstate New York. Maggie Fox was 14 and her sister Kate 11 when they came to public attention due to a series of rapping that occurred in their modest frame house. The Fox sisters maintained that they could communicate with the dead through rappings. The two sisters became famous and traveled from city to city giving demonstrations of their abilities. The experiences of the Fox sisters marked the birth of what would eventually become known as Spiritualism. The sisters became mediums of international fame and Spiritualism spread like wildfire throughout the United States and Europe.[140] Soon, many others claimed that they were also able to call up spirits. Although the industrial revolution and materialism were emerging, contacting spirits did not seem especially strange at that time. This was in part due to the fact that many families had children who succumbed to childhood diseases before the advent of vaccines. Families naturally wanted to know what happened to their loved ones. What followed was a spiritual movement that encompassed millions not only in America but in Europe. The spirit world was open to anyone who could communicate with it.

Paranormal phenomenon caught the attention of scientists who examined and researched many famous psychics and mediums in the late 1800's. In 1882, a group of scientists founded the Society for Psychical Research (SPR) in London. Three years later, the American Society for Psychical Research was founded in Boston, Massachusetts by the elite of the academic world. The society investigated countless people advertising themselves as mediums. More importantly, they sponsored vast amounts of research into thought transference, automatic writing, dream recalls and communication with the dead. In 1886, the SPR published *Phantasms of the Living* containing hundreds of corroborated reports involving spiritual communication. By the late 1800's the United States was home to thirty thousand so-call mediums, and in Philadelphia there were over three hundred "magnetic circles" (gatherings with a medium) convening on a regular basis. Anomalous mental capacities were thoroughly in vogue, and séances, where mediums purported to facilitate the appearance of the dead to commune with the living were a popular social event.[141] Some mediums were found to use tricks and deception while others were believed to have genuine psychic powers. Years later, the Rhine Research Center in North Carolina brought a statistical and laboratory approach to the study of extrasensory perception (ESP). In addition, the Parapsychological Association (PA) carries out scientific and scholarly study of telepathy, clairvoyance, psychic healing and precognition. Other well-known paranormal research organizations include: the Paranormal Network, the Monroe Institute, the Center for Fundamental and Anomalies Research and the Alliance Studying Paranormal Experiences. All have brought spiritual reality one step closer to the earth.

A new age spiritual movement has been intensifying and expanding substantially since the turn of the millennium on the foundation of the mediums of the 19th and 20th century. Many of today's enlightened spiritualists are those whose backgrounds include Christianity, Hinduism, Islam and Buddhism.[142] Besides believing in the continuous existence of the soul, spiritualists believe in the divine parenthood of God, the family of mankind, and the interconnectedness of spirits, angels and the creation. Many of the ideas are elements of older traditions in both Eastern and Western philosophies. Researchers estimate that New Agers number as many as 10 million to 20 million worldwide and constitute 12 to 15 percent of the U.S. population.[143] As a result, the new age movement has affected and influenced literature, arts, business, music, crafts and education throughout the world.

As time went by, more and more mediums and psychics functioned as human pipelines for the transmission of messages from unseen sources. They have special ability to communicate with the spirits of men, women, children and even animals. Their primary mission was to console people whose love ones passed into the spirit world prematurely. Through corroboration from the spirit world, they have helped thousands of grieving relatives attain closure after a loved one has died.

Many mystics, mediums and visionaries have been involved in open channeling, acting as a vehicle for sources beyond themselves. Aboriginal, indigenous and shamanistic cultures have always accepted the process of mediumship. They were familiar with the subtler levels of reality as if was an everyday routine. Channelers go into a trancelike state while remaining fully conscious of all that is around them. The simplest people became instruments or vessels for channeling. Whereas psychics and trance medium are often just conduits of information, mystics possess the wisdom to know what to do with the information.[144]

Mediums use a meditative state to connect to spirit. They are able to raise their frequency vibration far above the average person. Mediums can raise their spiritual vibration to understand messages from the spirit world much like radios and cell phones send and receive signals. Mystical traditions have often referred to highly spiritual individuals as possessing higher vibrations than normal people.[145] Some use automatic writing, which is the process where the hand appears to move by itself to scribble words. Others use a form of telepathy, receiving thoughts from spirit in their minds. By sensing which thoughts are theirs and which are the spirits, they can pass on the information received with much clarity. Often not only thoughts can be transmitted, but also images and feelings. During this form of telepathy, most mediums merge their own aura (energy field) with the energy field of the spirit.

More recently, remote viewers demonstrate unusual clairvoyant ability by traveling back and forth in time. They can bi-locate, traveling great distances in the twinkling of an eye simply by thinking themselves there. Remote viewing experiments have shown that they can accurately describe distant locations.[146] Their travels, even through solid objects, allow them to travel through different dimensions. They possess supernormal abilities to modify reality through bypassing conventional rules of nature and familiar laws of physics. Many political leaders have used these remote viewers for military or scientific research. They are called psychic spies and often hidden from the public. And almost without exception they kept their abilities a secret out of fear of damaging their professional reputations.[147] Millions of people are reluctant to admit their unusual psychic experiences publicly.[148]

For years, no matter how much they tried to kill off ghosts and voices, out of this world communication continued unabated. The question was not if there were reports of the paranormal but how to intermingle them with current religious and scientific reasoning. To the distaste of both scientist and clergyman—united in their aversion for all things superstitious—the popular fascination with the spirit world spread like a grass fire.[149] Telepathy, precognition, postcognition, psychokinesis, psychic healing, out of body experiences, near death experiences, after death communication and mediumship all pointed to psychic capabilities. Their descriptions of the earth paled compared to the spirit world.[150] The trees, flowers, the water and all life is said to be much more beautiful than on earth. The spirit world was this world made perfect, including emotional harmony and the unimaginable happiness that accompanies blissful love. Neither conventional science nor traditional religion had the ability or desire to handle this unknown territory.

Sudden impressions or intuitions of a strong message coming through are usually the first sign of an ESP experience. Many spontaneous ESP experiences occur as messages from the dead. They help bridge the gap between the spiritual and physical worlds by connecting families with deceased love ones on the other side. The most common information delivered through psychic experiences are messages of consolation, last goodbyes, words of advice, information needed to complete unfinished business or to right an old wrong.[151] The messages from mediums were meant not just to enrich people but to help them open their minds to the truth of the spirit world.

Mediums have also helped in the development of science and technology. Everything that is accomplished in manifestation as an idea on earth begins in the spirit world.[152] For that reason many of the richest and most influential people in history were recipients of mediumistic readings. It is now clear that such scientific luminaries as Thomas Edison and Nikola Tesla were give trance readings by Edgar Cayce, as were the engineers at RCA, IBM, Delco and the president of Goodyear Tire and Rubber Company. The inventor Mitchell Hastings credited Cayce with helping him to develop the FM radio. Innovative electronic technologies designed by Cayce in trance are now used in almost every large hospital and airport in the world.[153] Andrew Jackson Davis, known as America's first prophet, went into a trance day on a daily basis and dictated visions of other planets, heaven, angels, afterlife realms, and the spiritual mechanics of the entire universe.[154] Over his lifetime, Andrew Jackson Davis predicted the creation of the typewriter, the automobile, the airplane and the birth of spiritualism.[155] In 1863, Jules Verne began writing with intriguing detail about things to come. Within a single novel, *Twenty Thousand Leagues Under the Sea*, he foresaw the full development and impact of the submarine, the aqualung, fully automatic rifles, television and space travel.[156]

The reality of spirit world is increasing due to the work of clairvoyant mediums and the internet. One example is the new-birth.net website (http://new-birth.net/contemporary messages.htm) where thousands of important spirit world messages have been revealed. Everybody can decide for themselves their authenticity. Some departed mediums that have made great spiritual contributions include:

- Emanuel Swedenborg
- Kate & Maggie Fox
- Arthur Ford
- George Meek
- Anthony Borgia
- Edgar Cayce
- Mina Crandon
- Jean Dixon

- Ruth Montgomery
- Daniel Douglas Home
- Eileen Garrett
- Lenora Piper
- Jane Roberts
- Andrew Jackson Davis
- Alan Kardec
- Helena Petrovna Blavatsky
- Carmine Mirabelli
- Rosina Thompson
- Suzy Smith
- Geraldine Dorothy Cummins
- Elizabeth Blake
- Rosemary Brown
- Carl Wickland
- Ivy Northage
- Gladys Osborne Leonard
- Eusapia Palladino
- Harold Sherman
- Leslie Flint
- Etta Wriedt
- Eva Carriere
- Eileen Jeanette Garrett
- Arthur Findlay
- John Cambell Sloan
- Maurice Barbanell
- Helen Duncan
- Elwood Babbitt
- Estelle Roberts
- George Chapman

- Grace Cook
- James E. Padgett
- Stefan Ossowiecki

Well-known living mediums seem to improve over time. These include:

- James Van Praagh
- John Edwards
- Sylvia Browne
- Rosemary Altea
- April Crawford
- J.Z. Knight
- Jach Pursel
- Allison Dubois
- Lisa Williams
- Colin Fry
- Derek Acorah
- Doreen Virtue
- Gillian Kemp
- Suzane Northrop
- Jon Klimo
- Kevin Ryerson
- George Anderson
- Anne Puryear
- Jean Foster
- Johanna Carroll
- Concetta Bertoldi
- John Holland
- David Edward Thompson
- Uri Geller

- Josiane Antonette
- Gordon Smith
- Mary T. Browne
- Steve Holbrook
- Theresa Caputo

All have brought back important information for the benefit of humanity.

———◆———

PREMONITIONS

The five spiritual senses are often referred to as the sixth sense. One of primary gifts in the development of the spiritual senses is premonition. Premonition and precognitive abilities, although presumably new, are old as recorded time. This ability to listen to one's sixth sense or second sight transcends the physical senses. Premonitions are usually about the major events in the distant future although they could be about close at hand individual affairs. Some are associated with world events but many are about mundane issues. In the past, individuals who could see the future in detail were considered shamans, prophets and oracles and they occupied places of honor in their societies.[157] Whether it is for direction, healing or protection, guidance from a higher source has always encouraged and sustained man. For as long as anyone can remember, humanity has had an innate desire to know what is yet to come.

People are accustomed to believe that knowing the future is not possible yet surveys have shown that in most countries, more than half the population are reportedly having psychic experiences (PSI). Much of what is reported as news can be something that was previously anticipated by those who could "see" the future. Many people are surprised to find they have paranormal abilities. We all possess the ability to access the future.[158] Many people can

unconsciously pre-recognize the future and make decisions based on this "new" information. Acquiring information about future or distant events challenges our beliefs
of time and space. This "mindsight" is also used in remote
viewing so that distant mind to mind communication can
take place. Using the second set of senses has been helpful in exploring, hunting, warfare, business, sports and
even in creating new innovations. Gradually more people
are discovering that they can detect events before they occur. There are a significant number of accounts of people
claiming they have experienced premonitional dreams, but
in the "civilized" world this notion is not given much credibility.

Unfortunately, premonitions or precognitive visions
tend to be of tragedies with unhappy events outnumber-
ing happy ones by a ratio of four to one.[159] Precognitive
thoughts of unforeseen events occur in dreams regularly.
By tapping the unconscious mind, precognitive information can be accessed. Solid breakthroughs have occurred
in premonition research that was totally unanticipated.[160]
Warnings of accidents or illness are often stunningly accurate in pictorial detail.[161] Numerous examples of prophecies and premonitions are contained in religious scriptures
which has strongly affected culture.

Among indigenous people, the experience of journeying outside the body is regarded as entirely natural and
even routine.[162] There's a theory that prehistoric people
were able to survive their harsh environment because they
had highly developed psychic skills. Humankind gradually
lost these abilities as civilization became more complex. In
the past, conscious foreseeing of future events was com-

mon, but today people watch events unfold on television or learn about them from the internet. A great deal of PSI research has validated unconscious foreknowledge of future events. Psychic power is our heritage and with practice we can recapture the talent and enhance our natural abilities.[163] Today, this renewed ability is used to help track down criminals, find mineral deposits, discover archaeological sites, spy on enemy targets and diagnose medical conditions.

Precognitive dreams make possible the gaining of information about an upcoming event prior to its happening. Without it, people can be blindsided by unforeseen disasters or misfortune. The response to a nocturnal premonition can certainly affect one's future. Literature is filled with example of people who were able to use their precognitive glimpses of the future to avoid disasters. There are instances where individuals correctly foresaw the crash of a plane and avoided death by not getting on or who had a vision of their children being drowned and moving them out of harm's way just in the nick of time. Many lives have been saved by listening and understanding premonitions.

On the other hand, dismissing a premonition can be risky. Lives might be lost by not heeding an unconscious premonition. A feeling or belief that something is going to happen is usually indistinguishable from a premonition. Many people go into hiding and do not talk about forewarnings for fear of exposing themselves to unkind ridicule. There were nineteen documented cases of people who had precognitive glimpses of the sinking of the Titanic.[164] Numerous premonitions are now known to have preceded both the Kennedy assassination and the Civil War. Statistical studies of

U.S. railroad accidents found that significantly fewer people took trains on accident days.[165] The four airplanes involved in the tragedies of 9/11 were only 21 percent full suggesting large cancellations and no shows may have saved many passengers' lives. Even animals which have keener senses than humans seem to have a precognitive ability. The December 26, 2004 tsunami found no evidence of dead animals in the Sri Lanka's Yala National Park. Those humans who paid close attention to animal behaviors fared best during the tsunami.[166] The *Final Destination* movies show how to avert death after receiving premonitions of what is going to happen.

Humankind has an instinctual need to survive by understanding ahead of time what will happen. Precognitive phenomenon is like seeing a shadow that is casting an outline of future events around us. The spirit world, as the causal world, sees and knows what is going to happen on the earth. The human consciousness has a natural ability to transcend time and space. Just as the laws of motion and electromagnetism work well in either direction, the unconscious can be aware of events occurring in both the spiritual causal world and the resultant physical world simultaneously. Since future knowing has been demonstrated empirically, society should adapt its activities accordingly. Today's physics allows for the existence of paranormal phenomena such as telepathy, precognition and psychokinesis.[167] What actually transpires is not always definite, but definitely possible. People's inclinations and reactions can and does affect the outcome of future events. The eventual outcome depends on man's free will or response. Yet when social pressure, technology or nonessential viewpoints get in the way, man's natural ability of intuition dwindles.

Many professions would rather their most talented people be silent about any premonitions out of fear they'd appear crazy. This conflict between fitting in and being psychic can paralyze someone's innate freedom. However, as more people learn to listen to their inner self, the unexpected will no longer be so unexpected.

DREAMS

Belief in the afterlife probably arose from dreams, since dreamers often encountered deceased relatives and friends. Instinctively, humanity has always sensed the importance of dreams. Whether it is a symbolic message or an omen of things to come, dreams have always caught people's imagination. Dream researchers hypothesize that the dream world is an alternative dimension, a parallel universe or the invisible spirit world. Either way, between this world and the next is the world of dreams. Dreams occur involuntarily yet many may have important significance. Although hard to recollect, most people dream several times a night. During sleep the body rests, and the blood circulation slows. It can be compared to the sediment settling to the bottom and clear water rising to the top. Then the original, clear mind can make contact with the good spirit world. This is why revelations usually come through dreams.[168] It is possible to move quite smoothly between worlds during sleep as we are not overloaded with physical activities. Usually when we go into deep sleep during the early portion of each night's rest, the astral body leaves the physical body but remains connected with the silver cord.[169]

The dream world is a kind of parallel universe where some people even live another existence when they go to sleep. The spirit body often travels during sleep.[170] Edgar Cayce commented that each and every soul leaves the body as it rests in sleep. Your astral body—your butterfly body can and does travel while your body is asleep.[171] In the dream state the mind is not shackled and is able to move between situations and probably events in the past and future with equal mobility.[172] There have been many instances when the conscious mind of man has been temporarily quieted through sleep that contact has been made between the soul of a departed one and our own inner consciousness. The result is a vivid dream impression, occasionally so real as to give a carry-over feeling that we have been in touch with the other world.[173]

Most people have no idea how influential dreams have been in the past and continues to be in the development of civilization. Dreams inspired virtually every spiritual tradition and mythology on earth. Religions have been born and molded via the dreams of prophets and writers.[174] The historical evidence of God warning and informing man through dreams is impressive. Joseph became prime minister of Egypt and Daniel became chief governor of Babylon for their ability to interpret dreams. In a dream God can reveal life-changing information and guidance, as He did in the Bible.[175] About fifteen prophetic dreams are recorded in the Old Testament. The birth of Jesus was surrounded by dreams to Joseph and the three wise men. Also documented is the ancient world's use of dreams in diagnosing and even in curing diseases.[176] The arts, the sciences, and technology have been greatly influenced by people who have made good use of their dreaming minds.

Modern man has forgotten how to interpret the symbol and metaphors in dreams. Dreams appear difficult to understand because of their symbolic meaning. However, when dreams are interpreted correctly both the conscious and unconscious mind becomes clear. Understanding how dreams have guided man's past, present and future is fundamental in understanding the human existence. From the earliest times dreams have been given significant attention by prominent rulers and simple people alike. Dreams exist for ordinary people to illuminate the path of the individual's life, as guidebooks for living, for making one's way through the day.[177] Common people have relied on dreams for their very survival especially in difficult times. Sometimes messages conveyed are ambiguous or unclear. The seers of ancient times professed the ability to foretell the future through dreams.[178] Tribal cultures are well aware of this fact, and shamanic traditions almost universally stress how important dreaming is in divining the future.[179]

Dreams see a larger purpose to life. In the past, people look to dreams for guidance and gave them much respect that is lacking today. They suggest how to conduct life and make decisions. The ancient civilizations cultural paths were guided by the internal illumination provided in dreams. Dreams, astrology and the occult have always aided mankind to understand the unknown. The current dream denying Western culture could benefit from dream elucidation to better improve communication with nature and with one another. Dreams not only enriched lives with new ideas but are agents for change. Notions of success, good fortune and status come to those who acquire this sacred knowledge. Consequently, the profound meaning inherent in dream life has been honored universally throughout history. It is not unusual for psychic dreams to be given during a dream state.[180]

Among the Greek gods, Aesculapius, an important health and healing god, was believed to have sent medical advice and cures in dreams. Greeks would journey to a temple, fast, perform rituals and sleep on a temple floor hoping that Aesculapius would show up overnight and offer up some advice. The Greeks wrote volumes about dreams including the oldest surviving dream dictionary, *Oneirocritica*. In ancient Egypt, dreams were thought to be messages from the gods. Professional dream interpreters set up temples all along the Nile to help people understand their dreams. In India, the Hindus developed the idea that this world is actually a dream and the 'real' world is somewhere else. The Aborigines of Australia and Native Americans of North America considered dreamtime an important guide to everyday life. In North and South America, the Aztecs and Incas indigenous cultures paid close attention to dreams. In Native American cultures, dreams have always been an integral part of the spiritual life of the community to teach, guide, heal and prophesy. Several Native Indian communities put particular emphasis on the medium of dreams as a channel to the supernatural. Only with the help of supernatural forces could a Native Indian hunt well, farm well, bring up children well, and if necessary, fight well. In Native American tribes, they would share their dreams with one another upon waking. In the world of the Native Indians, the dream is real.[181]

Dreams were seen as important for creative inspiration, spiritual guidance and even forecasting weather and hunting conditions. Culture was often defined in terms of their dreams and it dictated almost every aspect in their way of life. They considered the dream as the master of their lives.[182] A great dream is more to be desired than any material thing in life.[183] Unlike normal dreams in which the dreamer is primarily a passive participant, the lucid dreamer is able to control the dream in various ways—turn nightmares into pleasant experiences, change the setting of the dream, and/or summon up particular individuals or situations.[184] Lucid dreamers maintain full waking consciousness and are aware they are dreaming. They believed that it was not until one sleeps that the spirit truly wakes up.

The ancient Chinese, Japanese, Greeks, Egyptians, Hindus and Muslims all practiced dream cultivation and experienced astounding results. Traditional Chinese philosophy says that while you are sleeping, your spirit leaves your body for nighttime adventures. In some parts of Africa, dreams were considered as important as waking experiences and taken to heart. Dreams were when you close your eyes, but opened your mind. The psyche of man possesses a latent ESP capacity that is most likely deployed during sleep, in the dreaming phase.[185]

In many cultures the most profound insights into the fate of one's spirit has been attributed to soul travel during dreams. When a Native American boy is about thirteen years old, it was time for him to find out his life's purpose. He prepared to seek his vision in a dream. Without this successful vision quest, life would be a failure. With it, he will gain the right to an important career. In these native cultures, there is no separation between the waking state and the dream state.

Visiting these other worlds was a top priority for our ancestors.[186] The dream state is a direct means of communicating with departed loved ones. Oftentimes, deceased relatives and friends appear in dreams with messages. There are profound cultural, social and personal elements to the dream experience. Dreams are a powerful source of guidance from our psyche which helps us develop an individualized road map through the paths of our life. Understanding dreams helps to relate more intimately and effectively in family, social and occupational relationships. Dreams help counterbalance any limiting physical viewpoint accepted as true. Nightly dreams can serve as both a compass and guide to life's journeys.[187] Dream travel was used to find the source of healing, to commune with spirits, to gain insights and to rescue lost souls. Paying attention to dreams can benefit those around us because this is where truths are given.[188] By listening to dreams, a higher consciousness than the rational mind is attained. Most importantly, the appreciation of dream life deepens and enhances respect for the spirit world.

Dreams have not only led to scientific and artistic developments but have also served as channels for spiritual inspiration.[189] The fact that God and angels could speak to humankind in dreams verifies spirit intervention occurring through the process of dreams. From the beginning to the end of the Bible, dreams and visions played a vital role in communication between God and man. God spoke to Moses, saying, "If there be a prophet among you, I will…speak to him in a dream."[190] Most of the revelations in the Bible and other scriptures are given in dreams. Over seventy percent of the revelations recorded in the Bible are given through the medium of dreams.[191] The Bible often equates the appearance of an angel with a dream. The three wise men were warned in their dreams not to return to Herod. The Bible says in the last days, "I will pour out my spirit on all flesh, and your sons and daughters shall prophesy, and your young men shall see visions, and your old men shall dream dreams."[192] In Genesis, God gives notice to Abimelech in a dream warning him against taking Abraham's wife Sarah as his wife. God identifies himself and promises a wonderful covenant to Abraham, Jacob and Joseph in dreams. Saint Paul experienced the third heaven in a dream-like state. Virtually all of the major writers and church fathers in the first three centuries after Christ believed in the revelatory power of dreams. Sometimes, prophetic dreams foretelling events have raised grave concerns. Pontius Pilate's wife had a dream about Jesus where she told her husband, "Have nothing to do with that innocent man, because in a dream last night, I suffered much on account of him."[193] In Dante's *Purgatorio* a radiant guide named Beatrice chastises him for not heeding dreams in which she sought him for many years. Stories of the many martyrs and saints' lives are accented with dreams that foretold the future and provided meaningful encounters with God or his angels.[194]

The birth of Siddhartha Gautama, the Buddha, was similarly prefigured as Jesus' birth with a symbolic dream. Buddha told of dreams that caused his spiritual awakening. The first part of the Koran was said to have been received by the prophet Mohammad in a dream, and the holy city, Mecca, was promised to the faithful in another dream. Mohammed received his divine mission from a dream and he is said to have had great regard for dreams. The Hindu text, the Upanishads, recognized the importance of dreams. The ancient religions believed that dreams were the starting place of eternal life.

Prophetic dreams have also influenced political and military events throughout history.[195] The ancient Babylonians and Assyrians treated dreams with respect and had methods of decoding them. The Persian attack on Greece in 480 BC, Alexander the Great attack on Tyros in 332 BC, Hannibal's failed attempt to attack Rome and Julius Caesar's successful attack on Rome were all foreshadowed in dreams. The Roman Emperor Constantine had a dream where Christ appeared to him and told him to have the cross insignia which bore the inscription—"*Conquer By This*." The angel, Gabriel appeared to Muhammad in a dream and encouraged him to leave the city of Medina and lead an army to Mecca. After his triumphant conquest of Mecca, Islam spread quickly. Genghis Khan reportedly had two important dreams which inspired and sustained him through his impressive military career. During the conquest by Cortes, the Aztec ruler, Montezuma II ordered anyone having a dream about the fate of the empire to see him immediately. The mighty ruler who had been able to command tribute from much of Mexico was now paying tribute to his own citizens for their dreams.[196] Celebrated military commanders have been credited with highly developed abilities to travel beyond the body. Alexander the Great is said to have gone beyond his body to achieve a god's eye view of three of his battles.[197] Sitting Bull, the great Dakota leader, had a psychic dream of white men falling from the sky, before he defeated General Custard at Little Big Horn. Native American sorcerers were employed by both the French and English to "fly over" the enemy ranks during the French and Indian War. General George S. Patton frequently called his secretary to dictate battle plans that appeared to him in dreams.

Paranormal dreams represent a great advantage on one hand, but a great challenge to the rational mind on the other. When a dream tells which direction to go, modifying or not modifying one's behavior has its price. Many tribal cultures believe firmly in their dreams and act upon messages received in them. Advance dreaming gives warning signs to help avoid misfortune. In 1858, Mark Twain had a vivid dream which foretold his brother's death with extraordinary accuracy. Several people had written of their premonitory dreams of the sinking of the Titanic before it happen on April 14, 1912. There have been advanced dreams of airline disasters, volcanoes, earthquakes. It is not uncommon for people to dream of their death.[198] Less than a week before he was assassinated, Abraham Lincoln had a dream where he saw people sobbing over his coffin in the East Room of the White House. The 2007 movie, *Premonition*, tells the story of a wife that has a dream before her husband dies in a car accident. A forewarning usually comes in one form or another so a wise person can step out of its path to avoid the outcome.

Dreams foretelling the future are not as unusual as one may think. Hippocrates believed in prophetic dreams, diagnostic dreams and psychologically revealing dreams.[199] A great many men of science, poets, philosophers, musicians and others have declared they have received important ideas and suggestions in dreams. Descartes, the father of analytical geometry, believed that when he slept, he was visited by the 'Spirit of Truth.' Many authors, inventors, healers, artists and musicians have arrived at extraordinary ideas from dreams. Athletes, scientists and business people have also benefited from interpreting their dreams correctly. Dreams have been exceptionally helpful in the world of new innovations. All the major discoveries that are of service to the earth-plane have come, and always will come from the spirit world.[200] Elias Howe had a dream that showed him where to put hole in the sewing machine needle. Arthur Stilwell, one of the great railroad barons of the 19th century often took his inspiration from dreams. He was concerned that his respectable investors would consider him crazy if he revealed that he was laying railroad track according to plans given to him in his dreams.[201] He said that he had no doubt that these messages came from the spirit world. Frederick A.Von Kekule had been attempting for some time to solve the structure of the benzene molecule. He fell asleep and began to dream of atoms flitting before his eyes, forming various structures and patterns. His dream imagery of a benzene molecule with alternating double bonds revolutionized organic chemistry. Einstein declared that his theory of relativity of time dawned on him as he awaked from sleep one morning. The Russian chemist, Dimitri Mendeleev, dreamt of the Periodic Table of Elements when he fell into an uneasy sleep. Nobel Prize winning physiologist and pharmacologist Otto Loewi received his prize winning experiment in a dream.[202] America's foremost inventor, Thomas Edison, used to get some of his ideas while sleeping. Edison had a habit off catnapping between long hours at work. This frequent entry into this unconscious state has been said to be the key to many of his patented inventions and innovations. Many people to-day are unaware that the highly developed technological products around them are a result of dream-inspired accomplishments.

Dreams have also fueled the imagination of performers and composers throughout history.[203] Mary Shelley's *Frankenstein* was conceived from a dream. Robert Louis Stevenson dreamed the storyline of *The Strange Case of Jekyll and Hyde*. Chaucer was inspired to write *The Nun's Tale* from a dream and Charles Dickens gains the ideas for many of his characters and plots from dreams. John Lennon and Paul McCartney of the Beatles often woke up in the middle of the night with music and lyrics that later became great hits. Many authors have increased their literary productiveness and even reported breaking through writer's block while asleep. Dreams have supplied many writers with creative ideas and energy for writing stories. Robert Louis Stevenson described the central role of dreaming and dream-like states in his creative process in his essay "A Chapter on Dreams."[204]

Dreams have also affected history. Before the American Civil War, Harriet Tubman led hundreds of slaves to freedom by means of an "Underground Railroad." Her amazing feats were guided by specific dreams and premonitions, through which she learn about safe houses, river crossings and friendly helpers she had never previously known.[205] She never lost a single "passenger." After weeks of mediation, Gandhi had a dream which suggested that the people of India suspend their usual business activities for twenty-four hours and devote that time to prayer and fasting. The resulting nonviolent mass strikes of 1919 marked a turning point in India's effort to achieve self-determination.

Sigmund Freud, the first modern psychologist to explore the meaning of dreams, felt that dreams were a cover-up for something else. Freud's *Interpretation of Dreams* was written to help deal with mental illness. Although Freud's legacy forged a neurotic sexual link with dream imagery, his analysis of how symbolic elements of a dream must be examined, paved the way for science of dreams. Carl Jung, in contrast, observed that dreams are not difficult to understand at all, but are clear expressions of our very own nature that mean exactly what they say. His explanation of the synchronicity of dreams opened up new doors of telepathy through dreams. Jung thought that dreams not only exposed hidden conflicts or problems but they offer hints about the future. His concept of the collective unconscious—in which we all inherit common beliefs and understanding—is still studied today. As a result, more psychiatrists began studying the paranormal elements occurring in their patients dreams. Universities and medical centers have set up dream laboratories to evaluate psychic, ESP and telepathic dreams.

Recalling the particulars and identifying their meaning is crucial to understanding the unconscious dream side of life. Dreams often confront the dreamer with issues never previously considered. Interpreting the imagery can be a daunting task for the novice. Dreams serve as a manual or a map to navigate through the daily challenges of life. They are the most direct source of consistent guidance available for a life filled with problems. For this reason, it is important to understand dreams as something closer to nature and rooted in a far greater intelligence than the waking consciousness. When the physical body sleeps, the spirit body temporarily withdraws from it, while still remaining connected to it by an unbreakable cord. This cord is a veritable life line between the spirit body and the physical body. The spirit will gravitate towards the sphere which its earthly life, so far has entitled it to enter. The spirit will thus spend part of the lifetime of the earthly body in spirit lands.[206]

Dreaming shows unequivocally that the soul is active even when the body is asleep providing additional proof of man's immortality. It is very natural for dreamers to make contact with the dead. Some spirits need time or the right conditions to come into someone's dream. When you set your intention to have contact with the afterlife, you are both focusing on the essential vibratory signature of the individual whom you seek communication and also seeking to raise your own earthly frequency to be closer to that of the inhabitants in the afterlife.[207]

When there is a mutual base of yearning and love, contact through dreams comes about sooner or later. Dreaming allows not only the living to initiate communication with the departed but the deceased to be in touch with the living on earth. Dreams help to heal wounded relationships that can be a source of much needed forgiveness and closure. Visits by the dead in dreams have been described in cultures around the world for thousands of years.[208] Dreams with messages from the dead cut out the use of mediums as middlemen.

Just as dreams assist us for life's challenges, they also prepare us for conditions of life after life. Your dreamgate might take you into other life experiences that are relevant to you—from the past, from the future, or from parallel worlds.[209] Soul journeying is the undisclosed secret to knowledge of the spiritual world. A face-to-face encounter with death through a dream can fill someone with new passion and zeal for life. This close encounter with death instills courage to brave our deepest fears. Conscious dreaming are adventures where one can discover new places and knowledge. It brings keen awareness of a larger reality.[210] It is not a morbid preoccupation but instead frees man to live fully and creatively. The skills of conscious dreaming help people approach the last stage of life with confidence, possibly to discover extraordinary places which might be seen again after dying. If we are able to separate the dream state from the world of physical reality, we would also be able to recognize the moment of final separation of the spirit from the material body at the moment of death.[211] Probably the most amazing part of dreaming is that it is preparation for the challenges of the journey after physical death.[212] Through conscious dreaming, it is possible to explore the conditions of the one's afterlife. When we sleep we wake up on this side, when we die we wake up on the other side.[213]

Precognitive dreams are the most common source of ESP in the average person's life. Of over 7,000 spontaneous cases of ESP studied in the United States, nearly two-thirds of the cases were dreams, and a similar proportion holds true in one thousand cases examined in Germany.[214] Whether it is helping police solve mysteries, predicting the future or discovering a technological breakthrough, dreams have brought a greater awareness of the future.

Dreams, often mysterious, communicate important messages. Dreams "see" things not seen before.

Dreams make us face something about ourselves that might be blocking us from moving forward. Repetitive dreams are probably telling us to wake up and listen.[215] Dreams are particularly effective because there is no outside interference or inner censoring. They can help develop abilities far beyond the ordinary. The majority of people are thrilled to visit dream lands, to experience another dimension of life. Dreams are the main road to the unconscious and a great source of wisdom and guidance. If everyone listens, they may even point the way to a new civilization of peace and love.

TRANSCOMMUNICATION

Before radio, television, cell phones and the internet, few would have believed that the silence around them could be filled with signals and sounds only awaiting the proper instrumentation to make them alive. Through advances in technology, much of the invisible has been revealed. Mankind simply lacked the devices to be informed of their existence. Most of the light and sound waves go by without being seen or heard. Man's physical sight can only see a very narrow band of wavelengths of the light spectrum. There are sound waves at vibrational frequencies beyond the range of the human ear that only dogs can hear. These normally invisible sights and unheard sounds have a most important bearing on the question of life after death.[216] Other dimensional spectrums are also undetectable to human senses. Up until now, contacts from the next world has gone unnoticed because of a similar lack of awareness. What is "out there" is a vast ocean of waves and frequencies.[217] Recently, innovative electronic media devices have brought new information from the spirit world.

Electronic voice phenomena (EVP), Instrumental Transcommunication (ITC) and Direct Radio Voices (DRV) perceive the voices and pictures from people that have crossed over. The technical devices or instruments used by ITC and EVP experimenters include audio recorders, radio receivers, telephones, video recorders, television and computers, all of which "behave irregularly." During trans-communication, voices, images, and messages of varying quality, sometimes excellent, come apparently from "no-where." There are hundreds of experimenters throughout Europe and America involved in transcommunication. Each researcher is apparently establishing contact with other ranges of consciousness, including the dead.[218]

The Association for Voice Taping Research was founded in Germany in the 1970s. The next decade ushered in the American Association of Electronic Voice Phenomena, which provided a system for classifying the quality of sound from various EVP messages. In 1992, the International Network for Instrumental Transcommunication (ITC) was set up with the intent of intelligent, capable men and women to solve problems in our world with help and support from Beyond.[219] The first clear spirit voices came through radio sounds in 1985; the first spirit phone call came in 1986; the first clear television images from the astral world also came in 1986; computer contacts began in 1988 and fax in 1993.[220] Unfortunately, messages originating from beyond the earth via telephone, computer or fax are not adequate enough to make clear to humanity the reality of the spirit world. Most of the recordings of messages from the spirit allow conversations of the departed with their loved ones on earth. The voices that have come through said they were in another dimension and that one time they had lived on the earth. The phenomenon is spontaneous and cannot always be recreated under laboratory conditions.

One of the main goals of the most comprehensive ITC communications appears to be an attempt to contribute to the expansion of human consciousness, by conveying to us information of high ethical content that breaks with conventional human values.[221] The aim was to not only relieve grieving relatives, but to support discoveries that could benefit mankind. The ability to harness psychic powers from the spirit world could supply the technology to build an ideal world. In addition, ground-breaking artistic, musical and literal masterpieces could enhance modern day culture. Crimes fighting would be taken to a new level as potential criminals would realize their actions would be reported to the authorities in advance. In fact, communicators from the next life have already said that mankind should critically examine their values and ways of thinking implying that prevailing human concepts are filled with falsehoods. It was fear of death, boiling over into our social systems that had shaped our businesses, nations, and sciences into materialistic and hostile life forms that are wearing heavily on our planet.[222] They are the unfortunate consequence of our deeply rooted materialistic education and values which are extremely difficult to wipe out because they have become an intrinsic part of our mental universe.[223] Once harmony, respect and purity of purpose are achieved between the spirit and the physical world, many new inventions and far-reaching discoveries will be sent through to the earth. The day will assuredly arrive, and a torrent of new inventions will come pouring through from the spirit world to your world.[224] This new knowledge can be used to influence the world to move toward greater equality, justice and peace.

We have entered the age where the existence of the spirit world can be scientifically proven.[225] When this happens, the world will accept enthusiastically the beginning of a new era in which the life of the spirit will be revealed.[226] It is just a matter of time until more physical evidence attests to these truths. Many mediums have foreseen that dependable two-way communication with the spirit world will be established in the fullness of time. The departed are simultaneously building an instrument to enable them to speak directly to the people on earth.[227] The frequency of vibrations used by spiritualists and mediums will be vital to build a viable spirit world machine. It will make communication in a very wide range, so that many more people will be able to come in touch with the spiritual world. These devices to locate the spirit world will share incredible insights from the next world. The most obvious result will be that the deceased will emphasize that they are not dead, only existing on another plane. Thus, the needless and destructive fear of death will be removed, as well as the deep concern over the passing of a loved one.[228]

Our minds are already like radio stations—we're sending vibrations every time we concentrate on our loved ones and when we send them our love. [229] Religion and science will in the end join together in proving not only the existence of man's soul but the continuity of life beyond the grave.[230] In the future, when death has been scientifically proved to be the gateway to another life, all fear of death will be removed from the consciousness of mankind.[231] Funerals will be something to look forward to, not dreaded. For the first time, with mechanical assistance, communication with realms beyond the earth will be attainable. Those with scientific understanding will have the same knowledge of the afterlife as those with spiritual conviction. No longer can a political system fail to recognize its citizens as far more than one-lifetime, soulless cogs in a materially-oriented world, who face personal extinction at death.[232] The concrete means of intercommunication between the physical and spiritual world will be a source of great comfort and happiness. All things received will be given to be used for unselfish purposes. There will be a continuous exchange of good will and ideas between the physical and spiritual world to stimulate mankind to new heights.

Until recently, most spirit researchers were regarded with ridicule, suspicion and even humor. Yet it seems the desire of man to know the truth about spirit world never ends. In 2012, the John Templeton Foundation awarded a $5 million grant to the University of California at Riverside to research the question of life after death. This Immortality Project is expected to answer the perennial question of whether or not a person can survive bodily death. Establishing rapport with the beyond has always enchanted the masses as seen by the growing number of movies and TV shows of psychic phenomena, paranormal and ghostly events. Current day popular media and internet sites reflect the tendency to emphasize the paranormal.

It seems the attraction for the supernatural never ceases to exist.

REINCARNATION

Reincarnation, the idea that people are born into more than one physical body, is a well-known concept to explain the evolution of the soul. Reincarnation believes that every human soul gradually evolves toward spiritual perfection through the means of assuming a new physical body after the death of its previous physical body, in an indeterminate series, sometimes extending through millions of such embodiments.[233] The belief in reincarnation can be found in many of the ancient religions and continues to be present in modern times. The idea of reincarnation has appeared throughout history, including Plato and the ancient Greeks, Hindus and Buddhists in Asia, various West Africans, some Native Americans and even some groups of early Christians.[234] It is well-known that karmic reincarnation figures prominently in Buddhism and Jainism. The philosophy teaches that the spirit cannot be released from the wheel of life until it reaches the final stage of development, called Nirvana. Accordingly, souls have the opportunity to progress to the ultimate goal of perfection only when they are incarnated as human beings again and again. Thus, spirits seek out human bodies in which to be reincarnated, in hopes of a chance to right wrongs and make progress on the path.

The concept of reincarnation is persuasive because of man's innate desire to improve and live forever. The concept of making progress to become better across successive lifetimes gives great comfort to someone trying to make sense out of life. Having reincarnated from a past lifetime gives a remote explanation for some curious things that happen. An individual soul brings with it all the accumulated memories of what happened to it in past lives in order for it to progress. Since we are of the lineage of our forebears, all of us are historic reincarnations of our ancestors.[235] The law of karma holds the belief that we must reap the consequences of our actions in previous lifetimes. The need to repay karma parallels the need to compensate for sins or restore any mistakes make during the physical life. With karma the person who leads a good life will be rewarded with a comfortable existence next time, an evil person will be punished with a hard life of misery.[236]

At first reflection, the evidence for reincarnation is convincing as some patients under regression therapy talk unmistakably about past lives. Past-life therapy through hypnosis recalls many verifiable memories from previous life spans. Regression therapy employs hypnosis to urge clients to travel back in time into possible past experiences. It seems on first observation that the person may retain or recover the memory of other life experiences. There are correlations between the descriptions of memories of an apparent past life and research done with regard to that described past life. Subsequent events and situations that unfold reflect the dilemmas and conflicts faced by their counterparts of the past. Therapists and hypnotists who practice past-life regression are inclined to believe that these people came back in another body. Often these past life stories relate to and even explain current problems. Past-life phenomenon, interlife regression and shared memories all point to a cycle of going from lifetime to lifetime. The idea that after their life review a spirit decides that they want to restore or accomplish something has some credibility. Hindus believe that, like a chain, each life is connected to the past and to the future. Buddhism holds to a casual connection between lives produced by karma, although one is not the same person from one life to the next. The implication that life on earth is a repetitive spiritual journey is very peculiar considering the great majority cannot remember their past lives. Reincarnation after reincarnation, the slate of individual consciousness gets wiped absolutely clean. In fact, there is much reluctance for any of these intelligences to come back to the chaotic world of today.[237]

Many spirits do have a desire to do better if they had a chance to inhabit physical life again. There is often unfinished business in the life of the soul—business that can only be worked out on the earth plane.[238] As a result, the idea of reincarnation gives spirits the hope of eventual success at overcoming their problems and moving forward.[239] The belief that soul keeps learning lessons and needs to continually evolve to a higher state is a common aspiration. The goal is to fulfill life so that there is no need to come back.

The methodology of reincarnation has been mystifying as there is not a fully reasonable theory to explain how reincarnation works. Some of the actions of the previous lives help to explain the current state of affairs. Yet, no single explanation can justify all the cases. Some unanswered questions include: Does everyone reincarnate and when does it stop? What part of the soul returns and where and how is one reincarnated? [240] If the concept of returning to life is accurate, why can't we remember our past lives? Reincarnation cannot stand up to man's collective logical mind, there are only outlines of a theory, based on the assumption that consciousness continues to exist after a person dies and can attach itself to a developing fetus, bringing memories, emotions and even traumas with it.[241]

Parapsychological researchers have provided suggestive evidence through exploring past life memories that reincarnation occurs. However, upon further examination, these "past life memories" are only the memories of dead people who remain attached to the living. Many have had a "déjà vu" experience of having been there before. Déjà vu occurs as a residual effect of being in touch with many spirits and their memories on the earth. You then think you remember your past.[242] The spirit that is cooperating with them is so close, that for a brief second, they take over the person's body and has the experience of allowing that person on earth to share it with them. Déjà vu elucidates this principle of close cooperation of a spirit with a physical person. The idea of reincarnation is a misunderstanding and a misinterpretation of the phenomenon demonstrated by the temporary residence of an alien spirit in the body of an earthly being.[243] Hence, your vague, eerie sense of having done something before is oftentimes your experiencing the memories of a spirit who actually did that thing and who may be working with you or who is otherwise connected with you in some way.[244] We inherit the emotional responses, the trusts and distrusts, the likes and dislikes of spirits cooperating with us. Studies of reincarnation are mostly from same-family, same area and same religion circumstances. Psychiatrists and psychologists patients who study pre-birth memories found that patients are able to tap into the memories of their relatives and ancestors.[245]

Undeniably, the possibility of re-entry into the womb of another fetus is conceptually incoherent from a logical standpoint. The idea that one soul can inhabit numerous physical bodies not only defies logic, it goes against the main tenets of the Abrahamic religions. The notion of reincarnation is not only implausible but it is ludicrous.[246] There exist no undisputed and generally acknowledged data establishing reincarnation. Past-life memories recovered through hypnotic regression are notoriously unreliable. Figuring out how many times who goes where is a dilemma of gigantic proportions. In addition, the argument that reincarnation is not compatible with the population explosion remains effectively unanswered.[247] A human soul is not designed, or suited, for inhabiting many different bodies, but is uniquely matched to its own physical body.[248]

This theory of taking many lifetimes to work out karma should be replaced with a more logical and complete system that can explain how spirits develop after they die. The system of returning resurrection where spirits grow in conjunction with another person's physical body provides the necessary explanation. Spirits who could not completely mature during their earthly life usually return to people on earth who share the same lineage or mission as they had during their lifetime and cooperate with them. Since spiritual growth does takes place on the earth plane, it would be logical to assume that individuals have to make use of another body to accomplish their responsibility. Human beings that have shed their physical body can only continue spiritual growth by returning and working with people on earth who still have their own physical bodies. Man must work through physical and emotional problems on earth.[249] Spirits can neither grow nor be resurrected apart from a physical self. The spirits of all that have passed from the physical plane remain about the plane until their development carries them onward or are returned for their development here.[250] The distinction is the method although the goal is the same—the growth of the spirit man to perfection.

We all must learn certain attitudes with the physical state.[251] As spirits return and render guidance and support to particular individuals on the earth, these spirits qualify to receive some of the vitality elements from the earthly person's physical body; on this basis, these spirits can continue to grow spiritually in the spirit world.[252] A spirit who returns to the earth for his resurrection may seek a counterpart among the earthly people of the religion in which he believed during his earthly life. The living assist the dead by shouldering the burden of their unfinished business and resolving it.[253] When a spirit helps an earthly person to fulfill their responsibilities, that person will not only fulfill their responsibility but also the mission of the spirit who has helped him. They enable earthly men to see many facts in the spirit world in a state of trance, give them the gift of prophecy, and inspire them spiritually.[254] In this way, descendents can resolve their ancestors' wrongdoings. As Hebrews 11:39-40 makes clear, "And all these, though, well attested by their faith, did not receive what was prom-ise, since God had foreseen something better for us, that apart from us they should not be made perfect." Since the earthly people are, in a sense, the second coming of these guiding spirits, they may think they are their reincarnation. Spirits can enjoy the benefits of resurrection by descending to earthly people and cooperating with them. By assisting people of faith living on the earth to fulfill their missions, the spirits may complete their missions at the same time.[255] Those who are involved in the works of good spirits enjoy an increasing sense of peace and righteousness. Therefore the earthly man sometimes takes on the name of the spirit man and frequently appears to be the reincarnation of the spirit man in order to accomplish the missions which they left unfulfilled in their earthly lives.[256] Consequently, the spirits of people who died before they could reach spiritual maturity during their earthly life can only be resurrected by returning to earth and completing their unaccomplished responsibility through cooperation with earthly people. In effect, they are resolving their unfinished business to allow themselves to be liberated and move to a higher level.

It is difficult to grasp the concept how a spirit evolves after leaving their physical body, without understanding the concept of returning resurrection. People who see the external manifestation of this phenomenon of returning resurrection are prone to interpret it as reincarnation. In dreams, it is not uncommon to travel in time and experi-ence the memories of other lives, especially one's ances-tors. Traveling clairvoyants like Swedenborg who visited the spirit world often and saw the situation there did not believe in reincarnation. Seasoned astral travelers that have control of their out of the body experiences also find nothing in the afterlife exploration that points to reincarnation. Many competent mediums have experienced directly the collaboration of spirits to accomplish their goals.

In review, soulful development and advancement is a continuous process. The fundamental error of reincarnation is believing that spiritual growth must occur through a succession of inhabiting different mortal bodies. It is impossible for a soul with a spirit body to enter the human body of another human being. A soul can never be separate from its spirit body as it is not originally designed or suited to inhabit many different physical bodies. This fact alone is sufficient to make clear that there are not repeated incarnations. Spiritual growth takes place in the context of each human person having one physical incarnation, not repeated mortal incarnations. If karmic restitution or atonement is necessary beyond one's lifetime, it is carried out not via further lifetimes of the same individual in different bodies but rather through cooperation with different individuals across succeeding generations. This small distinction makes a world of difference.

GOD

There is something in the human mind that needs to communicate with a higher power. Yet, as a collective, humanity has not recognized the presence of God within their midst. The problem is that human beings are ignorant of God's divine love. God and man are supposed to be one but man denies this fact and consequently feels rejected. God has been continually trying to speak to man through his soul, sharing with him inner wisdom and spiritual power. That is because God is the true parent of all mankind and desires only to experience love and joy together with his children.

CONCLUSION

Many people consider the subject of life after death unthinkable, unspeakable and even taboo. When it does arrive for family and friends, everybody's stress levels go through the roof. The bereaved at funeral services are typically traumatized due to insecurity of the departed's future. Usually family and love ones are in deep despair and are looking for closure after the passing. This is all the result of unpreparedness for the journey to the next world.

Modern traditions do not provide important education about life after death. In public schools the teachers keep the children busy cramming non-essential information into student minds.[257] Governments, major institutions, and even religions have assisted in the spiritual bankruptcy of mankind. Today's leaders are only guiding people through an external organizational framework. There is actually an untrue state of affairs that exists on earth because of ignorance of the spirit world. Humanity will soon realize the blindness and stupidity that the world puts forward by not telling their citizens about the spirit world. Ironically, many of the world's problems can be solved by revealing the spiritual law of advancement through service to others.[258]

Contemporary thinking does not encourage metaphysical reflection. A pleasant concept of death is not the mainstream perception and as a result the matter is usually avoided. It is not fashionable in science to consider any phenomenon that seems to support the idea of a spiritual reality.[259] The explosion of scientific knowledge has buried man's spiritual way of thinking. Materialistic and humanistic thought such as scientific socialism have disconnected man from his eternal destiny. As a result, many people have difficulty accepting death as a doorway to something new.

While not everyone believes in immortality, most of the world's people believe in some form of afterlife. Learning to accept psychic ability as a normal part of human consciousness is the first step to bridging the gap between the physical world and the spiritual world. Due to humanity's developing ESP backed by empirical data, the invisible spirit world is now becoming the new world of reality. More and more people are seeing and perceiving it through the five spiritual senses. Through studying the testimonies and experiences of people that have "been there", the spirit world will become more real. Human beings do not appreciate that they are inherently spiritual beings and consequently that their futures hold unimaginable possibilities for growing to more completely resemble God.[260]

If men knew what a happy and beautiful place the spirit world is, they would look forward to the day of departure from this world to the next.[261] Those who have had a near death experience or who have had an out of the body experience know that life is continuous and unending. NDEs and OBEs remind us of a common spiritual thread and destiny. A realm of joy, light and love is yearning to be revealed. By studying near death experiences, powerful evidence now exists for the existence of an afterlife.

Shared deathbed experiences with angels and departed relatives are almost common with medical personnel and relatives sharing dying patients' visions. Learning what people experience in those final hours will shatter any mistaken narrow-mindedness about the conditions of life after death. Many are not aware that death in the physical world is merely a birth into the other dimensions of life.[262]

The spirit world is urgently trying to prepare people on earth for their eventual death and entry into that world. Earthly life is only a training ground for life after death. Ironically, the ancients taught that the life of the spirit world is the true life and that life in the physical plane is only a learning experience.[263] When someone "wake ups" in the spirit world after death, they will feel much more alive. It is no longer tied down to the body and can travel freely at will.[264] Yet the percentage is still inexcusably low of people who come to spirit world with any knowledge of their new life and of the spirit world in general. All the countless souls without this knowledge have to be taught, taken care of, and helped with their difficulties and perplexities. Disgracefully, the average earth-dweller has no notion what kind of place the next world can possibly be, usually because he has not given much thought to the matter. "Why were we not told about this before we came here?" they cry. [265] The most widespread reaction of those who have died is to rush back to the earth plane to tell those they have left behind all about it. It is the shame of the earth that so many souls should arrive here in the spirit world in woeful ignorance of what lies before them.[266]

Death from natural disasters, diseases and wars has always brought spiritual matters back to the center of life.

Understanding that life continues after the physical body expires is the greatest tonic against fear. Instead of being life's enemy, death is the benevolent extension of life on earth. Anyone who realizes this one truth could save themselves a lot of unnecessary worry. Death is the fulfillment of our purpose on earth.[267]

The era of the spirit world is imminent. A shift in perception along with a subtle awareness is all that is needed.[268] Avoiding the subject of death and the next life is not serving anyone. Many of the personal and social problems that face humanity—drug and alcohol abuse, depression, suicide, gang violence, religious strife, racism and so on—could be greatly affected by powerful common spiritual experiences.[269] The invisible substantial world does not have to be perceived as a strange, eerie place beyond imagination. Humanity will stop living in fear of death once they know of the spirit world's character, splendor and benefits. The most beautiful aspect of the rebirth of man as a spiritual being is the awakening of his eyesight so that he may see other dimensions and may travel among the astral cities and fields and the beautiful mountains of the higher astral worlds at will.[270] Death relocates us to a finer, more peaceful world.[271] Simply put, the spirit world has a much superior vision for bettering the earthly world. The universal force will guide man to live a life corresponding to the highest realm in spirit world. Sooner or later, the whole earth will understand this.

There are increasing amounts of information about mysticism, psychic travels, ghost stories and the paranormal that are getting harder to explain. Soon the scientific proof of the existence of the spirit world will impact human history more than any other discovery or invention. It will bring an evolutionary thrust toward higher consciousness for all humanity.[272] The course of learning and development only starts on earth but continues in the next life. All the gold in the world does not buy this kind of knowledge. If truth be told, the real meaning of life on earth can best be understood by learning *All About the Spirit World*.

EPILOGUE

SUICIDE IS NOT THE ANSWER

Every year one million people in the world successfully commit suicide. Suicide is tragic for both the victim and their survivors. Often it is performed in a moment of unbearable emotional distress or total hopelessness.[273] What is unfortunate is that the society's imbalances put so much unnecessary stress on people's lives that they think suicide is the only way out. When one loses confidence to find their goal and purpose in life, they may take their life. Only someone in pain and confusion would end their life. How many people are restlessly wandering around half-crazy, agonizing over whether to live or die, questioning life, and committing suicide?[274]

In the grand scheme of things, life's biggest problems are almost insignificant. Earthly problems are never as meaningful on the other side. An even bigger contradiction is that if you die, your problems will end. Someone who takes their physical life doesn't really die. One cannot "kill" oneself. A person who fails to cope with everyday problems does not escape by suicide. Leaving the physical body behind does not eliminate struggles in the consciousness that transcends death. Suicides experience the same inner pain that led them to take their lives.[275]

It is good to recall here that God does not judge suicides and does not consign them to nether gloom; rather, the suicides themselves have created their own dark predicaments in response to their own self-judgment.[276] Sometimes suicides find themselves trapped in an isolated, dark, depressing and desolate environment.[277] Suicides suffer in these hellish places and have difficulty moving to a pleasant, higher dimension. A long, hard and lonely struggle lies ahead before this soul achieves the level on which it would have arrived by natural death.[278] Still there is always help if someone just reaches out for it, either here or in the next world. In the spirit world, they are helped to heal and to learn to love themselves in a good way. Educating people about the bigger picture can help avoid many suicides.[279] We all are responsible for one another, both on earth and in the next life. Learning *All About the Spirit World* can literally make a world of difference.

Movies Depicting the Spirit World

A Christmas Carol
A Guy Named Joe
A Matter of Life and Death
Angels in the End Zone
Angels in the Outfield
City of Angels
Constantine
Dead Like Me: Life After Death
Defending Your Life
Down to Earth
End of Days
Final Destination 1,2,3,4,5,6
Finger of God
Flatliners
Furious Love
Gabriel
Ghostbusters
Ghost
Ghost Dad
Ghost Rider I,II
Ghost Ship
Ghost Town

Heart and Souls
Heaven Can Wait
Hereafter
Here Comes Mr. Jordan
It's a Wonderful Life
Jacob's Ladder
Legion
Made in Heaven
Michael
Oh, God
Oh, God Book 2
Paranormal Activity 1,2,3,4
Poltergeist
Premonition
Saved by the Light
Soul Survivors
Spirit World 1, 2
The Devil Inside
The Ghost and Mrs. Muir
The Heavenly Kid
The Lovely Bones
The Other Side
The Prophecy
The Sixth Sense
The Exorcism of Emily Rose
The Haunting in Connecticut
What Dreams May Come
White Noise

TV Shows Depicting the Spirit World

Afterlife TV
A Gifted Man
Angel
Angels in America (HBO miniseries)
Charmed
Dead Zone
Fact or Faked: Paranormal Files
Fallen
Ghost Adventures
Ghost Hunters
Ghost Stories
Ghost Whisperer
Ghostly Encounters
Highway to Heaven
Life After Medium
Long Island Medium
Medium
My Ghost Story
Neverwhere
Paranormal State
Psychic Kids
Psychic Detectives

Sightings
Supernatural
The Case of ESP
The Unexplained
Topper
Touch by an Angel
Talking Dead
The Haunted
The Other Side

INTERNET REFERENCES

INTRODUCTION
The Rhine Research Center. At http://www.rhine.org/

Is There Proof the Spirit World Exists?—Channeling Erik. At http://www.channelingerik.com/is-there-proof-the-spirit-world-exists/

Home | Life Beyond Death. at http://www.lifebeyonddeath.net/home

TLC Family 'Is there life after death?' at http://tlc.howstuffworks.com/family/life-after-death.htm

HowStuffWorks 'How Dying Works'. at http://science.howstuffworks.com/environmental/life/human-biology/dying.htm

Encyclopedia of Death and Dying. at http://www.deathreference.com/

Introduction: Death and Dying: Merck Manual Home Edition. at http://www.merckmanuals.com/home/fundamentals/death_and_dying/introduction.html?qt=&sc=&alt=

108

What happens to the body as a person is dying?—Curiosity. at http://curiosity.discovery.com/question/body-as-person-dying

Spiritualism (beliefs)—Wikipedia, the free encyclopedia. at http://en.wikipedia.org/wiki/Spiritualism_(beliefs)

Spiritualism—Wikipedia, the free encyclopedia. at http://en.wikipedia.org/wiki/Spiritualism

New Age—Wikipedia, the free encyclopedia. at http://en.wikipedia.org/wiki/New_Age

Anthroposophy—Wikipedia, the free encyclopedia. at http://en.wikipedia.org/wiki/Anthroposophy

SPIRIT WORLD
Afterlife—New World Encyclopedia. at http://www.newworldencyclopedia.org/entry/Afterlife

The Spirit World. at http://www.intuitive-connections.net/2003/spirit_world1.htm

Immortality Project. at http://www.sptimmortalityproject.com/

life after death « 2012thebigpicture. at http://2012thebigpicture.wordpress.com/tag/life-after-death/

Afterlife Knowledge: The truth about life after death. at http://www.afterlife-knowledge.com/index.html

American Society for Psychical Research. At http://www.aspr.com/

Americans More Likely to Believe in God Than the Devil, Heaven More Than Hell. at http://www.gallup.com/poll/27877/americans-more-likely-believe-god-than-devil-heaven-more-than-hell.aspx

Out-of-body experience—Wikipedia, the free encyclopedia. at http://en.wikipedia.org/wiki/Out-of-body_experience

After-Death States—The Tibetan Buddhist and Spiritualist Views. at http://www.spiritualtravel.org/OBE/afterdeath.html

LightandLife.com—An Exploration of the Spiritual Universe. at http://www.lightandlife.com/

The Parapsychological Association. at http://www.parapsych.org/

Near death, explained—Neuroscience—Salon.com. at http://www.salon.com/2012/04/21/near_death_explained/

D.A Lascelles « News From The Spirit World. at http://newsfromthespiritworld.com/author/doggiepedia/

Spiritual Scientific Inc—The New Home of the Institute for the Scientific Study of Consciousness. at http://spiritualscientific.com/

Albert Taylor. at http://www.zoomper.com/Taylor.htm

Angels & Ghosts: Ghost Pictures, Angel Pictures, Angel & Ghost Stories. at http://www.angelsghosts.com/

Spirit World Research Center. at http://www.angelfire.com/planet/spiritworldresearch/index.html

Grant R. Jeffrey Ministries. at http://www.grantjeffrey.com/article/journey.htm

The FMBR—Where Science and Consciousness Produce Wisdom. at http://www.fmbr.org/

College of Psychic Studies | Home. at http://www.collegeofpsychicstudies.co.uk/index.html

About the Association for Transpersonal Psychology. at http://www.atpweb.org/about.aspx

About the Out of Body Experience (OBE) | The Monroe Institute. at http://www.monroeinstitute.org

Scientific evidence for survival of consciousness after death. at http://www.near-death.com/evidence.html

Life After Death. at http://lifeafterdeath.info/

Afterlife—Wikipedia, the free encyclopedia. at http://en.wikipedia.org/wiki/Afterlife

New study: What really happens when you die?—TODAY Health—TODAY.com. at http://today.msnbc.msn.com/id/33055601/ns/today-today_health/t/new-study-what-really-happens-when-you-die/#.Tz5h27SLUlg

Beyond The Mind-Body Problem | The Human Consciousness Project | The AWARE Study | Nour Foundation. at http://www.nourfoundation.com/events/Beyond-the-Mind-Body-Problem/The-Human-Consciousness-Project/the-AWARE-study.html

Mind Science Foundation. at http://www.mindscience.org/

Phantasms of the Living Cases. at http://www.iupui.edu/~peirce/writings/v6/Casesx.htm

Princeton Engineering Anomalies Research. at http://www.princeton.edu/~pear/

Insights Into the Afterlife. at http://www.unification.org/ucbooks/afterlife.html

The Out-of-Body Travel Foundation! at http://www.outofbodytravel.org/outofbodytravelhome.html

WORLD SCRIPTURE CHAPTER 6: Life Beyond Death and the Spiritual World. at http://www.unification.net/ws/intch6.htm

Visions of the Spirit World: Sang-hun Lee's Life in the Spirit World and on Earth Compared with Other Spiritualists' Accounts. at http://www.journals.uts.edu/volume-ii-1998/78-visions-of-the-spirit-world-sang-hun-lees-life-in-the-spirit-world-and-on-earth-compared-with-other-spiritualists-accounts.html

The Guild—Welcome to the Forge Website. at http://www.theforge.org/site/content.php

Institute of Noetic Sciences | Consciousness | Science | Spirituality | Wisdom. at http://noetic.org/

Intuition Network. at http://www.intuition.org/

The Division of Perceptual Studies—School of Medicine at the University of Virginia. at http://www.medicine.virginia.edu/clinical/departments/psychiatry/sections/cspp/dops/home-page

After-Death Communication (ADC): Hello From Heaven! by Bill and Judy Guggenheim. at http://www.after-death.com/

EHE Network Inner Page. at http://ehe.org/display/splash.html

Psi-mart.com—For all the readings and current information on paranormal activity. at http://www.psi-mart.com/home.php

The Association for Transpersonal Psychology promoting a vision of the universe as sacred. at http://www.atpweb.org/

Synchronized Universe. at http://www.synchronizeduniverse.com/

Journal of Scientific Exploration. at http://www.scientificexploration.org/journal/

FST: Spiritual Teachings: Life in the Spirit World, Part 1. at http://www.fst.org/sptwld1.htm

The Institute for Afterlife Research—Home Page. at http://www.mikepettigrew.com/afterlife/

Mrs. Padgett Tells of Her Experience of Leaving Her Physical Body and Going to the Spirit World. at http://www.fcdt.org/Publications/WHAYD/w_1_1_4.htm

Spirituality, Happiness, Health: Spiritual Science Research Foundation. at http://www.spiritualresearchfoundation.org/

GHOST RESEARCH SOCIETY. at http://www.ghostresearch.org/

A Wanderer in the Sprit Lands Index. at http://www.sacred-texts.com/eso/wsl/index.htm

Survival of Consciousness About Us. at http://www.survivalofconsciousness.com/about/about.html

http://www.afterlifeconference.com/

A Spiritual Journey—a start. at http://new-birth.net/journey.htm

Spiritworld.PDF. at http://new-birth.net/booklet/Spiritworld.PDF

CarolineDLarsen-My_Travels_in_the_Spirit_World.pdf. at http://new-birth.net/booklet/CarolineDLarsen-My_Travels_in_the_Spirit_World.pdf

Gone_West.pdf. at http://new-birth.net/booklet/Gone_West.pdf

Subaltern_Spirit_Land.pdf. at http://new-birth.net/booklet/Subaltern_Spirit_Land.pdf

Anthony Borgia-Heaven_And_Earth.pdf. at http://new-birth.net/booklet/Anthony%20Borgia-Heaven_And_Earth.pdf

Life_in_the_World_Unseen.pdf. at http://new-birth.net/booklet/Life_in_the_World_Unseen.pdf

http://www.divinelove.org/

http://www.messagesfromspiritworld.info/Speeches/LifeandDeath.html

Afterlife Forums—Welcome to AfterLife Forums. at http://www.afterlifeforums.com/

Immortality—Wikipedia, the free encyclopedia. at http://en.wikipedia.org/wiki/Immortality

NEAR DEATH EXPERIENCE

Michael Sabom—near-death experience research. At http://www.near-death.com/experiences/experts07.html

The Near Death Experience: Dr Bruce Greyson | TDG—Science, Magick, Myth and History. At http://dailygrail.com/Spirit-World/2009/5/Near-Death-Experience-Dr-Bruce-Greyson

What is a Near-Death Experience? at http://iands.org/what-is-an-nde.html

Near-death studies—Wikipedia, the free encyclopedia. at http://en.wikipedia.org/wiki/Near-death_studies

NDE Stories. At http://iands.org/nde-stories.html

IANDS—the most reliable source of information on NDEs. At http://iands.org/home.html

AFTER DEATH COMMUNICATION RESEARCH FOUNDATION (ADCRF). at http://www.adcrf.org/

Near Death Experience. at http://www.kktanhp.com/NDE_.htm

Life After Life: The Official Online Presence of Raymond A. Moody, M.D., Ph.D. at http://lifeafterlife.com/

Contents Page of Near Death Experiences. at http://aleroy.com/contents.html

HowStuffWorks 'How Near-death Experiences Work'. at http://science.howstuffworks.com/science-vs-myth/extra-sensory-perceptions/near-death-experience.htm

Near-death experience—Wikipedia, the free encyclopedia. at http://en.wikipedia.org/wiki/Near-death_experience

Near Death Experience Research Foundation (NDERF) with Evidence of the Afterlife and From Soul to Soulmate. At http://www.nderf.org/

Spiritual Travel—A Selection of Near-Death Experiences (NDEs). at http://www.spiritualtravel.org/OBE/neardeath.html

Near-Death Experiences and the Afterlife. at http://www.near-death.com/

Near-Death Experience Stories. at http://www.weboflove.org/neardeathexperience

A Study of Near Death Experiences. at http://www.aleroy.com/

PMH Atwater—near-death experience research. at http://www.near-death.com/experiences/experts05.html

ANGELS

Angel—Wikipedia, the free encyclopedia. at http://en.wikipedia.org/wiki/Angel

Inspirational Stories of Angels by Author Joan Wester Anderson—Guardian Angels—Angels Among Us. at http://joanwanderson.com/

Doreen Virtue | official Angel Therapy Web site. at http://www.angeltherapy.com/

Angel Names: Names of Angels. at http://www.angels-ghosts.com/angel_names

Welcome to Angels-Online, Stories of Angel Encounters, Miracles & Inspiration. at http://www.angels-online.com/

Seraphim—Encyclopedia Of Angels, Angel Names, Art, & Angelic Symbols. at http://www.seraphim.com/

You have reached the Center of Being…at http://www.centerofbeing.com/

Angels in art—Wikipedia, the free encyclopedia. at http://en.wikipedia.org/wiki/Angels_in_art

CATHOLIC ENCYCLOPEDIA: Angels. at http://www.newadvent.org/cathen/01476d.htm

I Believe in Angels | Heavenly Angels | Guardian Angels. at http://www.ibelieveinangels.com/

Your Angel Stories. at http://www.spiritual-encyclopedia.com/angel-stories.html

The Seven Archangels. at http://www.spiritual-encyclopedia.com/archangels.html

HEAVEN
Heaven and its Wonders and Hell From Things Heard and Seen by Emanuel Swedenborg. at http://www.swedenborgdigitallibrary.org/contets/HH.html

Heaven—Wikipedia, the free encyclopedia. at http://en.wikipedia.org/wiki/Heaven

Heaven—near-death experiences. at http://www.near-death.com/experiences/research18.html

What Will Heaven be Like? at http://www.godandscience.org/doctrine/heaven.html

Kingdom of God—Wikipedia, the free encyclopedia. at http://en.wikipedia.org/wiki/Kingdom_of_God

Important Truths that all mankind should know. at http://new-birth.net/stone.htm

HELL
Inferno (Dante)—Wikipedia, the free encyclopedia. At http://en.wikipedia.org/wiki/Inferno_(Dante)

Bill Wiese 23 Minutes In Hell Official Website. at http://www.soulchoiceministries.org/

Hell—Wikipedia, the free encyclopedia. at http://en.wikipedia.org/wiki/Hell

Heaven and its Wonders and Hell From Things Heard and Seen by Emanuel Swedenborg. at http://www.sweden-borgdigitallibrary.org/contets/HH.html

What Will Hell be Like? at http://www.godandscience.org/doctrine/hell.html

Three Contemporary Descriptions of Hell. at http://www.bukisa.com/articles/387436_three-contemporary-descrip-tions-of-hell

Hell-On-Line: About Hell, Texts, Images, Timeline, Glossary, Motif Index, Bibliography; Eileen Gardiner, editor. at http://www.hell-on-line.org/

The Truth About Hell. at http://www.av1611.org/hell.html

Descriptions of the Levels of Dante's Inferno. at http://4degreez.com/misc/dante-inferno-information.html

basic.theology.forums > The Eternal Reality of Hell. at http://www.basictheology.com/articles/The_Eternal_Re-ality_of_Hell/

Earthbound—near-death experiences. at http://www.near-death.com/experiences/research14.html

Christian views on Hell—Wikipedia, the free encyclopedia. at http://en.wikipedia.org/wiki/Hell_in_Christian_beliefs

Is Hell Real—Is Hell Real? at http://www.eternalhell.net/

Hell—LookLex Encyclopaedia. at http://looklex.com/e.o/hell.htm

Book of Devils and Demons The Ranks of Hell. at http://www.angelfire.com/realm/shades/demons/bookdevil-sanddemons/ranksofhell.htm

The reality of hell: stories of persons who visited hell and apparitions of the damned. at http://www.tldm.org/News8/RealityOfHell.htm

World Scripture—Hell. at http://www.unification.net/ws/theme044.htm

Hell—Theopedia, an encyclopedia of Biblical Christianity. at http://www.theopedia.com/Hell

St. Faustina's Vision of Hell. at http://www.divinemercysunday.com/vision.htm

Testimonies—To Hell and Back. at http://www.amightywind.com/hell/testimonies.htm

Hell is Real, I went there! by Jennifer Perez. at http://spir-itlessons.com/Documents/Jennifer_Perez/Hell_is_Real_I_Went_There_Jennifer_Perez.htm

Billions of People are Going to Hell! at http://www.jesus-is-savior.com/billions_of_people_going_to_hell.htm

http://www.spiritualtravel.org/OBE/mistaken-hell.html

GettingOut.PDF. at http://new-birth.net/booklet/Get-tingOut.PDF

Theistic Satanism—Wikipedia, the free encyclopedia. at http://en.wikipedia.org/wiki/Theistic_Satanism

Satanism—Wikipedia, the free encyclopedia. at http://en.wikipedia.org/wiki/Satanism

MEDIUMS
Centre for Fundamental and Anomalies Research. at http://www.c-far.org/index.html

The Monroe Institute | Explore Consciousness—Transform Your Life. at http://www.monroeinstitute.org/

Paranormal Network :: Enlightenment Awaits. at http://www.paranormalnetwork.net/

ParaNexus Anomalous Research Association | Paranormal Researchers | Paranormal Investigators | Hauntings, UFO Sightings, Alien Abductions, More. at http://www.paranex-

us.org/index.php?PHPSESSID=c9d0d1d64e7da75b921a2c
ed165b3cba;www

Berkeley Psychic Institute :: Berkeley Mission. at http://
www.berkeleybpi.com/

True Gospel Revealed Anew From Jesus. at http://www.
truthforallpeople.com/index.php?option=com_content&
view=section&id=5&Itemid=59

Divine Love Divine Truth—Home. at http://www.di-
vinelovedivinetruth.org/home

Emanuel Swedenborg—Wikipedia, the free encyclopedia.
At http://en.wikipedia.org/wiki/Emanuel_Swedenborg

JohnEdward.net | The ONLY Official Worldwide Website for
Psychic Medium John Edward. At http://www.johnedward.
net/

Welcome to the James Van Praagh Online Community ::
Welcome! At http://www.vanpraagh.com/index.php

True Deep Trance Psychic Channeling. at http://www.april-
crawford.com/index.html

Sylvia Browne—Spiritual Teacher and Psychic—join the Inner Circle today. at http://www.sylviabrowne.com/

Rosemary Altea. at http://www.rosemaryaltea.com/index1.
cfm

george anderson website. at http://www.georgeanderson.com/

Spiritual Medium, Author, Teacher, and Channeler of Saint Germain—Philip Burley | Philip Burley. at http://www.philipburley.com/index.html

Sherry Sherry Psychic Predictions Channel Medium Intuitve Readings. at http://www.sherrysherry.com/

Channeling | Channeling.net. at http://www.channeling.net/

Paranormal Research Society. at http://paranormalresearchsociety.org/

History of The Society for Psychical Research | Society for Psychical Research. at http://www.spr.ac.uk/main/page/history-society-psychical-research-parapsychology

Archives of the Journal of Parapsychology. at http://www.rhine.org/journalarchive.htm

Parapsychology.org—for answers to all your questions about parapsychology, here is the place to find Parapsychology, paranormal phenomena, paranormal psychology, paranormal phenomenon, psychic phenomena, lyceum, Psychokinesis, hauntings, neardeath experiences. at http://www.parapsychology.org/

LIFE IN THE WORLD UNSEEN. at http://anthony3741.tripod.com/

ANTHONY BORGIA: Medium for a "Dead" Priest. at http://website.lineone.net/~enlightenment/anthony_borgia.htm

Edgar Cayce' s A.R.E. at http://www.edgarcayce.org/

Sleeping Prophet—Who was Edgar Cayce? at http://sleepingprophet.org/

Society for Psychical Research. at http://www.spr.ac.uk/main/

Andrew Jackson Davis. at http://www.andrewjacksondavis.com/

Suzane Northrop—Heal The Loss of Loved Ones. at http://suzanenorthrop.com/

Home—Jean Foster. at http://www.jeanfoster.com/

Rev. Josiane Antonette » Matters of Spirit. at http://www.mattersofspirit.com/index.php

Psychic spiritual teacher & spiritual book author Johanna Carroll Biography About page. at http://www.johannacarroll.com/about.html

The Paranormal Network | Dimensions of the Unexplained. at http://mindreader.com/

BEST PSYCHIC DIRECTORY Read & Write Reviews Of Psychics & Psychic Mediums. at http://www.bestpsychicdirectory.com/

psychics usa. at http://www.americanassociationofpsychics.com/psychics_usa.htm

The Spirit World. at http://www.creativespirit.net/spiritworld/

P S Y C H O M A N T E U M The Other Side of the Mirror. at http://www.psychomanteum.com/

Scrying—Wikipedia, the free encyclopedia. at http://en.wikipedia.org/wiki/Scrying

Thoughts about consciousness, spirituality, psychic research at http://www.paranormalia.com/

The Psychic Times. at http://thepsychictimes.com/

Remote viewing—Wikipedia, the free encyclopedia. at http://en.wikipedia.org/wiki/Remote_viewing

Remote Viewing information and resource site. at http://www.remoteviewed.com/

Remote Viewing History Map. at http://www.remoteviewed.com/rvhistorymap.html

Maine Ghost Hunter's Society—Paranormal Glossary. at http://www.maineghosts.org/paranormal_glossary/

John Holland—Psychic Medium | Spirit communication and mediumship by spirit messenger and author John Holland. at http://www.johnholland.com/aboutjohn/faqs

LeslieFlint.com. at http://www.leslieflint.com/leslieflint.html

Survival Research Institute of Canada. at http://www.islandnet.com/~sric/

National Spiritualist Association of Churches, NSAC. at http://www.nsac.org/

List of Spiritualist Organizations—Association of Independent Readers and Rootworkers. at http://readersandrootworkers.org/index.php?title=List_of_Spiritualist_Organizations

Worldwide Mediums and Psychics Tarot Course. at http://www.worldwidemediums.net/

Official Site for Lily Dale Assembly | Lily Dale NY. at http://www.lilydaleassembly.com/

Spiritual Truth Foundation—Publishers of Silver Birch Books by Maurice Barbanell. at http://www.silverbirchpublishing.co.uk/

Circle of the Silver Cord—Proving the continuity of life after death. at http://circleofthesilvercord.net/

About The First Spiritual Temple: Gladys Osborne Leonard. at http://www.fst.org/leonard.htm

D.D. HOME—THE MAN WHO COULD FLY? at http://www.prairieghosts.com/ddhome.html

Extrasensory perception—Wikipedia, the free encyclopedia. at http://en.wikipedia.org/wiki/Extra-sensory_perception

Mediumship. at http://new-birth.net/mediumship.htm

The Truths of The Spirit World -. at http://www.meilach.com/spiritual/ramadahn_vol_1/index.htm

SSE Talks-Preliminary Investigation of a Spiritist Seance Group in Germany-Stephen Braude. at http://www.scientificexploration.org/talks/29th_annual/29th_annual_braude_investigation_spiritist_seance_germany.html

PREMONITIONS
Precognition—Wikipedia, the free encyclopedia. at http://en.wikipedia.org/wiki/Precognition

Prophecy—Wikipedia, the free encyclopedia. at http://en.wikipedia.org/wiki/Prophecy

Premonitions—how dreams can predict the future. at http://www.dreamsymbolism.info/adreampremonitions.php

Prophecy Update. at http://www.prophecyupdate.com/

Welcome to Prophecies. at http://www.prophecies.us/

Central Premonitions Registry | Level Beyond. at http://levelbeyond.com/2009/03/24/central-premonitions-registry/

Precognition—New World Encyclopedia. at http://www.newworldencyclopedia.org/entry/Precognition

Featured Web Site—Premonitions Registry. at http://www.intuitive-connections.net/issue3/webpremonitions.htm

Nostradamus Society of America. at http://www.nostradamususa.com/

Paranormal Research Organization (P.R.O.) An organization of professional paranormal invesigators. at http://www.paranormal-research.org/

American Psychic directory. The best psychics offering psychic reading. at http://www.americanassociationofpsychics.com/

Canadian Psychic directory. The best psychics offering psychic reading. at http://www.canadianassociationofpsychics.com/

UK Psychic directory. The best psychics offering psychic reading. at http://www.ukassociationofpsychics.co.uk/

Experiences of prophecy and premonition. at http://www.phenomenalog.com/en/?mod=categories&pg=1&id=15

Edgar Cayce 2012 Future End, Predictions Prophecies & Pole Polar Shift Changes. at http://www.umsonline.org/2012/2012Pgs/Who/Edgar-Cayce-2012-Future-End-Predictions-Prophecies.html

East Carolina University—paranormal. at http://www.ecu.edu/cs-acad/llp/paranormal.cfm

Precognitive dreams & premonitions—part 1—Spiritual.com.au. at http://www.spiritual.com.au/2011/07/precognitive-dreams-premonitions/

Psi Explorer. at http://www.psiexplorer.com/

Society for Scientific Exploration. at http://www.scientific-exploration.org/

Overview | About | Institute of Noetic Sciences. at http://noetic.org/about/overview/

GotPsi On-Line Psi Tests. at http://www.gotpsi.org/html/gotpsi.htm

ITP | The Institute of Transpersonal Psychology | Graduate Education Integrating Psychology and Spirituality since 1975. at http://www.itp.edu/

Welcome! Cognitive Sciences Laboratory, Anomalous Cognition Remote Viewing Scientific Research. at http://www.lfr.org/LFR/csl/index.html

Ganzfeld experiment—Wikipedia, the free encyclopedia. at http://en.wikipedia.org/wiki/Ganzfeld_experiment

Extrasensory Perception (ESP), Science, The Roots of Consciousness. at http://www.williamjames.com/Science/ESP.htm

http://www.crystalinks.com/prophecies.html

Premonition Dreams—Psychic and Medium Experiences. at http://www.psychic-experiences.com/real-psychic-story.php?story=5142

Contemporary Messages. at http://new-birth.net/contemporary_messages.htm

DREAMS
Ten Thousand Dreams Interpreted. at http://nickm.com/dreams/

An Online Guide To Dream Interpretation. at http://www.dreammoods.com/

Dream—Wikipedia, the free encyclopedia. at http://en.wikipedia.org/wiki/Dream

International Association for the Study of Dreams [IASD]. at http://www.asdreams.org/index.htm

ARAS—The Archive for Research in Archetypal Symbolism. at http://aras.org/

The Haden Institute. at http://www.hadeninstitute.com/summer-dream-conference/

The Academy of Dreams. at http://theacademyofdreams.com/

Dream interpretation—Wikipedia, the free encyclopedia. at http://en.wikipedia.org/wiki/Dream_interpretation

The Quantitative Study of Dreams. at http://www2.ucsc.edu/dreams/

Dream Interpretation | Dream Dictionary | Free Dream Meanings. at http://www.dreamforth.com/

Dreams Foundation: Dream Interpretation, Psychology & Research, Nightmares & Alternative Medicine. at http://www.dreams.ca/

Dream Analysis and Interpretation—Understanding Dreams. at http://www.sleeps.com/

Religion and Dreams | Dream Encyclopedia | dreamhawk.com. at http://dreamhawk.com/dream-encyclopedia/religion-and-dreams/

Visit Dream Laboratories. at http://library.thinkquest.org/C005545/english/activities/lab.htm

DreamScience.org—Robert J. Hoss, MS. at http://dream-science.org/

Top 10 Amazing Facts About Dreams. at http://listverse.com/2007/11/14/top-10-amazing-facts-about-dreams/

News Flash! at http://www.mossdreams.com/index.html

Psychic Dreamland—Free Interpreting Dreams And Control Interpret Dreams. at http://interpret-dreams.award-space.com/

The Dreamwork Institute Home Page. at http://www.studioforthehealingarts.org/Dreamwork%20Institute%20Main%20Page.html

Perchance to Dream. at http://www.kktanhp.com/Dream.htm

Welcome to Dream World and Spirit World. at http://dream-worldspiritworld.com/

Edgar Cayce on dreams. at http://www.near-death.com/experiences/cayce14.html

Dream Dictionary & Dream Interpretation. at http://www.experienceproject.com/dream-dictionary/

The Center for Creative Dreaming. at http://creativedreaming.org/

Apocalyptic Dreaming | Visions, revelations and discussions of the apocalypse, dreams of the end of the world. at http://www.apocalyptic.org/

Discover the Meaning Of Dreams using Personal Dream Analysis. at http://www.realmeaningofdreams.com/

Interpreting Dreams. at http://library.thinkquest.org/11130/

History of Dreams. at http://bahcecik.ipower.com/dreamcenter/history.htm

Famous Dreams—Dream Discovery and Dream Creativity. at http://www.brilliantdreams.com/product/famousdreams.htm

The History of Dream-Catchers has nearly been lost in the turmoil of cultural mixioing and destruction that followed on the heels of the European invasion. at http://www.realdream-catchers.com/dream-catchers/history_of_dream_catchers.htm

HowStuffWorks 'How Dreams Work'. at http://science.howstuffworks.com/environmental/life/human-biology/dream.htm

Our Dreaming Mind Home Page. at http://www.ourdreamingmind.net/

Dreams and Dream Interpretation: Edgar Cayce A.R.E. at http://www.edgarcayce.org/are/edgarcayce.aspx?id=2255

The Hierarchy of Dreams, and the Stages of Awakening. at http://www.spiritualtravel.org/OBE/hierarchy.html

Lucid dream—Wikipedia, the free encyclopedia. at http://en.wikipedia.org/wiki/Lucid_dreaming

Incubating Dreams Solves Problems. at http://www.intuitive-connections.net/2003/dreamincubation.htm

TRANSCOMMUNICATION
EVP & ITC History. at http://www.mikepettigrew.com/afterlife/html/evp___itc_history.html

homepage WorldITC. At http://www.worlditc.org/

Spiricom Report 1. At http://www.rodiehr.de/o_01_meek_spiri_000_007.htm

The research of G.W. Meek. At http://www.worlditc.org/h_07_meek_by_macy.htm

Association Transcommunication home. At http://atransc.org/

Electronic voice phenomenon—Wikipedia, the free encyclopedia. at http://en.wikipedia.org/wiki/Electronic_voice_phenomenon

Contacting the Dead in the Electronic Age. at http://para-normal.about.com/od/ghostaudiovideo/a/aa072604_2.htm

AFTERLIFE LAWYER PRESENTS THE EVIDENCE FOR LIFE AF-TER DEATH AND WHAT HAPPENS WHEN YOU DIE. at http://www.victorzammit.com/index.html

Instrumental Communication. TCI CUADERNOS. at http://www.abrigo.me/ITCJOURNAL/index.php?lang=en

Instrumental Transcommunication. at http://www.trans-communication.org/

The Scole Experiment. at http://www.thescoleexperiment.com/index.htm

Akashic records—Wikipedia, the free encyclopedia. at http://en.wikipedia.org/wiki/Akashic_records

SOUND CLIPS OF RECORDINGS OF PARANORMAL VOICES WITH MEDIUM LESLIE FLINT TELLING ABOUT AFTERLIFE—HEREAFTER—AMONGST OTHERS ACTRESS ELLEN TER-RY—DEATH—TERMINAL. at http://wichm.home.xs4all.nl/death_ra.html

aboutspiritfaces. At http://www.spiritfaces.com/02-about-spiritfaces.htm

Spirit world realms. at http://www.worlditc.org/f_02_macy_spirit_world_realms_0.htm

Voces de TCI. at http://www.abrigo.me/ITCJOURNAL/index.php?option=com_content&view=article&id=52&Itemid=58&lang=en

journals. at http://www.spiritfaces.com/04-journals.htm

Evidence for the Afterlife-Instrumental transcommunication. at http://www.victorzammit.com/evidence/itc.htm

Proof of afterlife. at http://www.worlditc.org/d_02_macy_more_proof_0.htm

EDISON ENIGMA: I HEAR DEAD PEOPLE « Clyde Lewis's Ground Zero Media. at http://www.groundzeromedia.org/edison-enigma-i-hear-dead-people/

Transcommunication Page. at http://www.ghostpi.com/What%20is%20ITC%20page.htm

Intuitive Times | Research. at http://www.intuitivetimes.ca/Spirituality/research/vol1-1communication.htm

Voices From the Shadows: The Voice Phenomenon of Parapsychology | Mysterious Universe. at http://mysteriousuniverse.org/2012/01/voices-from-the-shadows-the-voice-phenomenon-of-parapsychology/

REINCARNATION
Reincarnation—Wikipedia, the free encyclopedia. at http://en.wikipedia.org/wiki/Reincarnation

Resurrection—Wikipedia, the free encyclopedia. at http://en.wikipedia.org/wiki/Resurrection

IARRT—International Association for Regression Research & Therapies. at http://www.iarrt.org/

The Michael Newton Institute for Life Between Lives Hypnotherapy. at http://www.newtoninstitute.org/

Ken Ring's—Reincarnation and near-death experience research. At http://www.near-death.com/experiences/reincarnation02.html

Cryptomnesia—Wikipedia, the free encyclopedia. at http://en.wikipedia.org/wiki/Cryptomnesia

Revelation 20: Reincarnation is an oriental doctrine NTR:75. at http://new-birth.net/ntr/revelation20.htm

GOD
God—Wikipedia, the free encyclopedia. at http://en.wikipedia.org/wiki/God

Does God Exist? at http://www.doesgodexist.org/

God.com. at http://www.god.com/index.php?site=index&lg=en

Evidence for God from Science. at http://www.godandscience.org/

138

New Thought—Wikipedia, the free encyclopedia. at http://en.wikipedia.org/wiki/New_Thought

Church of Divine Science—Wikipedia, the free encyclopedia. at http://en.wikipedia.org/wiki/Church_of_Divine_Science

The Theosophical Society in America. at http://www.theosophical.org/

Religious Science—Wikipedia, the free encyclopedia. at http://en.wikipedia.org/wiki/Religious_Science

God : The Interview With God : Popular Screensavers : Inspirational Screensaver. at http://www.theinterviewwithgod.com/

Is This Your Brain On God? : NPR. at http://www.npr.org/templates/story/story.php?storyId=110997741

at http://www.conversationswithgod.org/

GodSpeaks.com. at http://www.godspeaks.com/intro.asp

The Dear God Project. at http://thedeargodproject.com/

God—near-death experiences. at http://www.near-death.com/experiences/research21.html

More Than 9 in 10 Americans Continue to Believe in God. at http://www.gallup.com/poll/147887/americans-continue-believe-god.aspx

The Gift of the Divine Love. at http://new-birth.net/dlindex.htm

Conversations with God—Official—Neale Donald Walsch. at http://www.nealedonaldwalsch.com/

EPILOGUE – SUICIDE IS NOT THE ANSWER
Suicide.org Websites—Suicide.org! at http://www.suicide.org/suicide-org-websites.html

Frequently Asked Questions for Rosemary Altea. at http://www.rosemaryaltea.com/faq/faq.cfm#7

Suicide—Do you need a reason…to live or to die? at http://areason.org/

Suicide Helplines. at http://www.suicide-helplines.org/

AFSP: Understanding and Preventing Suicide Through Research, Education and Advocacy. at http://www.afsp.org/

Psych Central: Suicide and Crisis. at http://psychcentral.com/resources/Suicide_and_Crisis/

SAVE | Suicide prevention information, suicide, depression awareness. at http://www.save.org/

SuicideHotlines.com—When You Feel You Can't Go On—Let Someone Know Your Pain. at http://www.suicidehotlines.com/

Suicide Prevention Help | The Friendship Letter | Global Web Directory. at http://www.suicidepreventionhelp.com/

National Suicide Prevention Lifeline—With Help Comes Hope. at http://www.suicidepreventionlifeline.org/

Veterans Crisis Line | Hotline, Online Chat & Text. at http://veteranscrisisline.net/

Samaritans Home Page. at http://www.samaritans.org/

Kristin Brooks Hope Center—Hopeline. at http://www.hopeline.com/

Suicide—YouTube. at http://www.youtube.com/watch?v=euV6nM8A1BE

Centre for Suicide Prevention (CSP)—Calgary, Alberta, Canada. at http://suicideinfo.ca/

Welcome to the Jason Foundation. at http://www.jasonfoundation.com/

Preventing Suicide Among LGBTQ Youth | The Trevor Project. at http://www.thetrevorproject.org/

SPRC | Suicide Prevention Resource Center. at http://www.sprc.org/

Suicide Prevention Resource Center (SPRC) | TeenScreen National Center for Mental Health Checkups. at http://www.teenscreen.org/about/support-endorsements/suicide-prevention-resource-center/

Discussions About Suicide. at http://www.meilach.com/spiritual/suicidetalks/index.html

http://usnews.msnbc.msn.com/_news/2012/06/08/12118030-report-16-percent-of-us-teens-have-considered-suicide?lite

Bibliography

Ahlquist, Diane, *The Complete Idiot's Guide to Life After Death* (2007). Penguin Group, New York, New York

Anderson, Joan Wester, *Where Angels Walk* (1992). Ballantine Books, New York

Arvey, Michael, *Reincarnation, Opposing Viewpoints* (1989). Greenhaven Press, San Diego, CA.

Baker, Sharon L., *Razing Hell* (2010). Westminster Knox Press, Louisville, Kentucky

Beliefnet, *The Big Book of Angels* (2002). St. Martin's Press and Beliefnet. Inc.

Berman, Philip L., *The Journey Home, What Near-Death Experiences and Mysticism Teach Us about the Gift of Life* (1996). Pocket Books, New York, NY

Betty, Stafford., *The Afterlife Unveiled* (2011). O Books. Winchester, United Kingdom

Blackmore, Susan, *Dying to Live, Near Death Experiences* (1993). Prometheus Books, Buffalo, NY

Blackwood, Gary L. *Paranormal Powers* (1999). Benchmark Books, New York

Bloom, Harold, *Omens of Millennium, The Gnosis of Angels, Dreams, and Resurrection* (1996) Riverhead Books, New York

Blum, Deborah, *Ghost Hunters* (2006) Penguin Press, New York

Borgia, Anthony, *Here and Hereafter* (1968). Psychic Press LTD. London, England

Borgia, Anthony, *Life in the World Unseen* (1954). Psychic Press LTD. London, England

Borgia, Anthony, *More About Life in the World* Unseen (1956). Psychic Press LTD. London, England

Briggs, Constance Victoria, *Encyclopedia of the Unseen World* (2010) Weiser Books, S.F., CA.

Brinkley, Dannion, *Saved by the Light* (1994). Wheeler Publishing, Hingham, MA.

Brinkley, Dannion, *Secrets of the Light, Lessons From Heaven* (2008). Harper Collins Publishers, New York, NY

Brown, Mary T., *Life After Death* (1994) Random House, New York

145

Brown, Sylvia, *The Other Side and Back, A Psychic's Guide to our World and Beyond* (1999) Penguin Group, New York

Brown, Sylvia, *Life on the Other Side* (2001) Penguin Group, New York

Butler, Tom & Lisa, *There is No Death and There Are No Dead* (2004). AA-EVP Publishing, Reno, Nevada

Budge, E.A. Wallis, *The Egyptian Book of the Dead* (2008). Penguin Books, New York, NY

Cardoso, Anabela, *Electronic Voices, Contact with Another Dimension?* (2010). O Books, Winchester, United Kingdom

Chopra, Deepak, *Life After Death, The Burden of Proof,* (2006) Harmony Books, New York

Cox-Chapman, Mally, *The Case for Heaven, Near Death Experiences as Evidence of Afterlife* (1995). G.P. Putnam's Sons, New York

Delaney, Ph.D., Gayle, *All About Dreams* (1998). Harper, San Francisco

Dening, Sarah, *Healing Dreams* (2004). Hamlyn, London, England

DeStanfano, Anthony, *A Travel Guide to Heaven* (2003). Doubleday, New York, NY

DeStanfano, Anthony, *The Invisible World* (2011). Double-day, New York, NY

Dossey, M.D., Larry, *The Power of Premonitions* (2009). Dut-ton, New York

D'Souza, Dinesh, *Life After Death, the Evidence* (2009). Regn-ery Publishing, Inc. Wash., D.C.

Eadie, Betty J., *Embraced by the Light* (1992). Gold Leaf Press, Placerville, CA.

Edward, John, *After Life, Answers from the Other Side* (2003). Princess Books, New York, N.Y.

Farb, Peter, *Man's Rise to Civilization* (1978) E.P. Dutton, New York

Feather, Dr. Sally Rhine and Schmicker, Michael, *Gift* (2005). St. Martin's Press, New York

Flaherty, Thomas H., *The American Indians, The Spirit World,*(1992). Time-Life Books, Alexandria, VA.

Fontana, David, *Life Beyond Death* (2009). Watkins Publish-ing, London.

Franchezzo, *Wanderer in the Spirit Lands* (1993). AIM Pub-lishing Company, West Grove, PA.

Freud, Sigmund, *The Interpretations of Dreams* (1950). Random House, New York

Gaulden, Albert Clayton, *Signs and Wonders, Understanding the Language of God* (2003). Atria Books, New York, NY.

Garfield, Ph.D., Patricia, *Creative Dreaming* (1995). Fireside Book, New York

Goldberg, Dr. Bruce, *Spirit Guide Contact Through Hypnosis* (2005). Career Press, Franklin, N.J.

Gordon, Ph.D., David, *Mindful Dreaming* (2007). The Career Press, Franklin Lakes, N.J.

Heath, Pamela Ray and Klimo, Jon, *Handbook to the Afterlife* (2010). North Atlantic Books, Berkeley, CA.

Hill, Napoleon, *Outwitting the Devil* (2011). Sterling Publishing, New York, NY

Holden, Janice Miner, Greyson, M.D., and Bruce, Holden, Janice Miner, *The Handbook of Near-Death Experiences, Thirty years of Investigation* (2009). ABC-CLIO, LLC, Santa Barbara, CA.

Holmes, Dr. Jesse Herman. *As We See It From Here* (1980). Metascience Corporation, Franklin, N.C.

Horowitz, Mitch. *Occult America, The Secret History of How Mysticism Shaped America* (2009) Bantam Books, New York

Hose, David & Takeko, *Every day God* (2000). Beyond Words Publishing, Hillsboro, OR.

Innes, Brian, *The Book of Dreams* (2007). Gramercy Books, New York

Jung, C.G., *Memories, Dreams, Reflections* (1963). Vintage Books, New York

Kelly, Henry Ansgar, *Satan, A Biography* (2006) Cambridge University Press, New York

Kirkpatrick, Sidney D., *Edgar Cayce, An American Prophet* (2000) Riverhead Books, New York

Kubler-Ross, MD., Elizabeth, *Death, The Final Stage of Growth* (1975) Simon & Schuster, New York

Kubler-Ross,MD., Elizabeth, O*n Life after Death* (2008). Celestial Arts, Berkeley, CA.

Lee, Sang Han, *Life in the Spirit World and on Earth* (2001) Family Federation for World Peace and Unification, New York

Long, M.D., Jeffrey, *Evidence of the Afterlife* (2010). Harper Collins Publishers, New York, NY

MacGregor, Rob, *Psychic Power* (2005). Barrons, New York

Macy, Mark, *Spirit Faces, Truth about the Afterlife* (2006). Red Wheel/Weiser LLC, S.F., CA.

Macy, Mark H., *Miracles in the Storm* (2001). New American Library, New York, NY

Mayer, Ph.D., Elizabeth Lloyd, *Extraordinary Knowing* (2007) Bantam Books, New York

Maxim, Ph.D., Elizabeth, *After Here, The Celestial Plane* (2010) Elizabeth Maxim

McElroy, Mark, *Lucid Dreaming for Beginners* (2007). Llewellun Publications, Woodbury, MN.

McManus, Jason (Editor), *Psychic Voyages, Mysteries of the Unknown* (1987). Time-Life Books, Alexandria, VA.

McManus, Jason (Editor), *Spirit Summonings, Mysteries of the Unknown* (1989). Time-Life Books, Princeton, New Jersey

McMoneagle, Joseph, *The Ultimate Time Machine* (1998) Hampton Roads, Charlottesville, VA.

Meek, George W., *After We Die, What Then?* (1987). Ariel Press, Columbus, Ohio

Meek, George W., *Healers and the Healing* Process (1977). The Theosophical Publishing House, Wheaton, IL.

Moen, Bruce, *Voyage to Curosity's Father* (2001). Hampton Roads, Charlottesville, VA.

Monroe, Robert A. *Journeys Out of the Body* (1971). Broadway Books, New York, NY

Monroe, Robert A. *Far* Journeys (1985). Doubleday, New York, NY

Monroe, Robert A. *Ultimate Journey* (1994). Doubleday, New York, NY

Moody, Jr. MD, Raymond A., *Life After Life* (1975). Mockingbird Books, Marietta, GA.

Moody,Jr. MD, Raymond & Arcangel, Dianne, *Life After Loss*, (2001) Harper, San Francsico

Moody,MD., Raymond, *Glimpses of Eternity, Sharing a Loved One's Passage From This Life to the Next* (2010). Guideposts, New York

Moody,MD., Raymong, *Paranormal,* (2012) Harper One, New York

Holy Spirit Association for the Unification of World Christianity, *Exposition of Divine Principle* (1996) HSA-UWC, New York, NY

Macy, Mark H., *Miracles in the Storm,*(2001) New American Library, New York

Meek, George. W., *After We Die, What Then,* (1987) Ariel Press, Columbus, Ohio

Miller, Lisa, *Heaven, Our Enduring Fascination With the After-life,* (2010) Harper, New York

Miller Ph.D, Sukie, *After Death* (1997). Touchstone, New York

Morse, M.D. Melvin, *Closer to the Light* (1990). Villard Books, New York

Morse, M.D., Melvin, *Transformed by the Light, the Powerful Effect of Near-Death Experiences on People's Live* (1992). Villard Books, New York

Moss, Robert, *The Secret History of Dreaming* (2009). New World Library, Novato, CA.

Moss, Robert, *Dreamgates, Exploring the Worlds of Soul, Imagination, and Life Beyond Death* (2010). New World Library, New York

Moss, Robert, *The Three Only Things, Tapping the Power of Dreams,Coincidence & Imagination* (2007). New World Library, Novato, CA.

Nelson,M.D., Kevin, *The Spiritual Doorway in the Brain, A Neurologist Search for the God Experience* (2011). Penguin Group, New York

Nuland, Sherwin B., *How We Die, Reflections on Life's Final Chapter* (1994). Alfred A. Knopf, New York

Parker, Julia and Derek, *The Complete Book of Dreams* (1998). DK Publishing, New York

Parker, Alice Ann, *Understand Your Dreams* (2001). H.J. Kramer, Novato, CA.

Pierce, Penny, *Dream Dictionary for Dummies* (2008). Wiley Publishing, Indianpolis, IN.

Piper, Don, *90 Minutes in Heaven, A True Story of Life and Death* (2004). Revell Publishing, Grand Rapids, Michigan

Pobanz, Kerry, *The Spirit-Person and the Spirit-World* (2001). HSA Publications, New York

Rinpoche, Sogyal, *The Tibetan Book of Living and Dying* (1993). Harper, San Francisco

Roberts, Arthur O., *Exploring Heaven* (2003) Harper, San Francisco

Roberts, James and Moustaki, Nikki. *The Divine Comedy:Inferno.,CliffNotes* (2001). Wiley Publishing, New York

Roleff, Tamara L., *Psychics, Fact or Fiction* (2003) Greenhaven Press, Farmington Hill, MI.

Sanford, John A., *Dreams, God's Forgotten Language* (1989). Harper, San Francisco, CA.

Schouweiler, Tom, *Life After Death, Opposing Viewpoints* (1990). Greenhaven Press, San Diego, CA.

Seton, Ernest Thompson, *The Gospel of the Redman* (2005). World Wisdom, Bloomington, IN.

Sherman, Harold, *You Live After Death* (1949). Merit Publications, NY

Shockley, Peter, *Reflections of Heaven* (1999). Doubleday, NY

Shroder, Tom, *Old Souls, The Scientific Evidence for Past Lives* (1999). Simon & Schuster, NY

Singh, Kathleen Dowling, *The Grace of Dying* (1998). Harper Collins Publishing, S.F. CA.

Spong, John Shelby, *Eternal Life: A New Vision* (2009) Harper One, New York

Stead, Estelle W., *The Blue Island* (2010). Mastery Press, Phoenix, AZ.

Swedenborg, Emanuel, *Afterlife, A Guided Tour of Heaven and Its* Wonders (2006). Swedenborg Foundation Publishers, Westchester, PA.

Talbot, Michael, *The Holographic Universe* (1991) Harper Collins Publishers, New York

Tart, Ph.D., Charles T., *The End of Materialism, How Evidence of the Paranormal is Bringing Science and Spirit Together* (2009). New Harbinger Publications, Inc., Oakland , CA.

Tompkin, Ptolemy, *The Modern Book of the Dead* (2012) Atria Books, New York

Tucker, MD, Jim B., *Life Before Life* (2005) St. Martin's Press, New York

Turner, Alice K., *The History of Hell* (19930. Harcourt Brace & Company, New York

Tymn, Michael, *The Afterlife Revealed* (2011). White Crow Books, Guilford, United Kingdom

Ullman, M.D.,Montague & Krippner, Ph.D, Stanley, *Dream Telepathy, Experiments in Nocturnal Extrasensory Perception* (2001). Hampton Roads, Charlottesville, VA.

Unification Thought Institute, *St.Augustine's Confessions from the Spiritual World* (2000) Sunghwa Publishing Co. Ltd., Seoul, Korea

Universal Peace Federation , *World Scriptures and the Teachings of Sun Myung Moon* (2007) Paragon House Publishers, St. Paul, Minn.

Van De Castle, Ph.D., Robert L. (1994). Ballantine Books, New York

Van Praagh, James, *Heaven and Earth, Making the Psychic Connection* (2001). Simon & Schuster Source, New York, N.Y.

Virtue, Doreen, *Divine Guidance* (1998). Renaissance Books, L.A., CA.

Walsch, Neal Donald, *Conversations with God, an Uncommon Dialogue* (1996). G.O. Putnam's Sons Publishers, New York, New York

Weise, Bill, *23 Minutes in Hell*, (2006). Charisma House, Lake Mary, Florida

Weiss M.D., Brian L., *Many Lives, Many Masters* (1988). Fireside Book, New York

Williams, Mary E., *Paranormal Phenomena, Opposing Viewpoints* (2003). Greenhaven Press, Farmington Hills, MI.

Wippler, Migene Gonzalez, *What Happens After Death* (1997) Llewellyn Publications, St. Paul, MN.

Wright, Vinita Hampton, *A Catalogue of* Angels (2006). Paracelete Press, Brewster.MA.

Zukav, Gary, *Soul Stories* (2000). Simon & Schuster, New York, NY

Endnotes

INTRODUCTION

1   Elizabeth Kubler Ross, M.D., *Death, The Final Stage of Growth* (Simon & Schuster, New York, 1975) 1

2   Sun Myung Moon, *Cheon Seong Gyeong* (Sunghwa Publishing Company, 2006) 624

3   Anthony Borgia, *More About Life in the World Unseen* (Psychic Press Limited, London, UK) 34

4   Sun Myung Moon, *The Divine Principle* (HSA-UWC publications, New York, 1973) 61

5   Anthony Borgia, *Here and Hereafter* (Psychic Press Limited, London, 1968) 21

6   Harold Sherman, *You Live After Death* (Merit Publications, New York, 1949) 10

7   Kerry Pobanz, *The Spirit Person and the Spirit-World* (HSA Publications, New York, 2001) 26

8   Sang Han Lee, *Life in the Spirit World and on Earth*) Family Federation, 1998) 26

9   Charles T. Tart, Ph.D., *The End of Materialism* (New Harbinger Publications, Oakland, CA., 2009) 244

10   Ptolemy Tompkins, *The Modern Book of the Dead* (Atria Books, New York, 2012) 172

11   Anthony Borgia, *Life in the World Unseen* (Psychic Press Limited, London, 1954) 70

12   Raymond Moody, *Paranormal,* (Harper One, New York, 2012) 213

PREMONITIONS

13   Mitch Horowitz, *Occult America* (Bantam Books, New York, 2009) 67

14   Charles T. Tart, Ph.D., *The End of Materialism* (New Harbinger Publications, Oakland, CA., 2009) 254

15   Elizabeth Lloyd Mayer, Ph.D., *Extraordinary Knowing* (Bantan Books, New York, 2007) 62

16   Melvin Morse, M.D., *Closer to the Light* (Villard Books, New York, 1990) 105

17   Michael Talbot, *The Holographic Universe* (Harper Collins, New York, 1991) 230

18   Raymond Moody Jr., MD, *Life After Loss*, (Harper, San Francisco, 2001) 170

19   Kevin Nelson, M.D. *The Spiritual Doorway to the Brain* (Penguin Group, New York, 2011) 216

SPIRIT WORLD

20   Sun Myung Moon, *The Divine Principle* (HSA-UWC publications, New York, 1973) 61

21   Sun Myung Moon, *The Divine Principle* (HSA-UWC publications, New York, 1973) 58

22   George W. Meek, *After We Die, What Then?* (Ariel Press, Columbus, Ohio,1987) 95

23   Pamela Rae Heath & Jon Klimo, *Handbook of the Afterlife* (North Atlantic Books, Berkeley, CA, 2010) 163

24   Anthony Borgia, *Life in the World Unseen* (Psychic Press Limited, London, 1954) 37

25   Pamela Rae Heath & Jon Klimo, *Handbook of the Afterlife* (North Atlantic Books, Berkeley, CA, 2010) 71

26   Pamela Rae Heath & Jon Klimo, *Handbook of the After-life* (North Atlantic Books, Berkeley, CA, 2010) 88

27   Anthony Borgia, *Life in the World Unseen* (Psychic Press Limited, London, 1954) 132

28   Pamela Rae Heath & Jon Klimo, *Handbook of the After-life* (North Atlantic Books, Berkeley, CA, 2010) 87

29   Pamela Rae Heath & Jon Klimo, *Handbook of the After-life* (North Atlantic Books, Berkeley, CA, 2010) 91

30   Sun Myung Moon, *The Divine Principle* (HSA-UWC publications, New York, 1973) 63

31   Chopa, Deepak, *Life After Death* (Harmony Books, New York, 2006) 5

32   Ptolemy Tompkins, *The Modern Book of the Dead* (Atria Books, New York, 2012) 204

33   Ptolemy Tompkins, *The Modern Book of the Dead* (Atria Books, New York, 2012) 261

34   Anthony Borgia, *Here and Hereafter* (Psychic Press Limited, London, 1968) 11

35   Michael Talbot, *The Holographic Universe* (Harper Collins, New York, 1991) 266

36   Michael Talbot, *The Holographic Universe* (Harper Collins, New York, 1991) 266

37   Ptolemy Tompkins, *The Modern Book of the Dead* (Atria Books, New York, 2012) 155

38   Lee, Dr. Sang Han, *Messages from the Spirit World* (Family Federation for World Peace and Unification, 2001) 24

39   Sun Myung Moon, *Cheon Seong Gyeong* (Sunghwa Publishing Company, 2006) 682

40   George W. Meek, *After We Die, What Then?* (Ariel Press, Columbus, Ohio,1987) 49

160

41   Sun Myung Moon, *The Divine Principle* (HSA-UWC publications, New York, 1973) 63

42   Pamela Rae Heath & Jon Klimo, *Handbook of the Afterlife* (North Atlantic Books, Berkeley, CA, 2010) 131

43   Sukie Miller, *After Death* (Touchstone, New York, 1997) 97

44   Pamela Rae Heath & Jon Klimo, *Handbook of the Afterlife* (North Atlantic Books, Berkeley, CA, 2010) 134

45   Pamela Rae Heath & Jon Klimo, *Handbook of the Afterlife* (North Atlantic Books, Berkeley, CA, 2010) 157

46   Pamela Rae Heath & Jon Klimo, *Handbook of the Afterlife* (North Atlantic Books, Berkeley, CA, 2010) 158

NEAR DEATH EXPERIENCE

47   Michael Talbot, *The Holographic Universe* (Harper Collins, New York, 1991) 270

48   Charles T. Tart, Ph.D, *The End of Materialism* (New Harbinger Publications, Oakland, CA., 2009) 229

49   Jeffrey Long, *Evidence of the Afterlife* (Harper, New York, 2010) 166

50   Harold Sherman, *You Live After Death* (Merit Publications, New York, 1949) 56

ANGELS

51   Melvin Morse, M.D., *Transformed by the Light* (Villard Book, New York, 1992) 27

52   Michael Talbot, *The Holographic Universe* (Harper Collins, New York, 1991) 269

53   Michael Talbot, *The Holographic Universe* (Harper Collins, New York, 1991) 250

54 Michael Talbot, *The Holographic Universe* (Harper Collins, New York, 1991) 249

55 Bruce Moen, *Voyage to Curiosity's Father* (Hampton Roads, London,2001) 145

56 Pamela Rae Hae & John Klimo, *Handbook to the Afterlife* (North Atlantic Books, Berkeley, CA. 2010) 57

57 David Fontana, *Life Beyond Death* (Watkins Publishing, London, 2009) 164

58 Constance Victoria Brigges, *Encyclopedia of the Unseen World* (Weiser Books,S.F., CA., 2010) 141

59 Michael Talbot, *The Holographic Universe* (Harper Collins, New York, 1991) 268

60 Mary T. Browne, *Life After Death* (Random House, New York, 1994) 8

61 Melvin Morse, MD., *Transformed by the Light* (Villard, New York, 2012) 83

62 Migene Gonzalez-Wippler, *What Happens After Death* (Llewellyn Publications, MN. 1997) 71

63 Michael Talbot, *The Holographic Universe* (Harper Collins, NY, 1991) 265

64 Universal Peace Federation,*World Scriptures & the Teachings—Sun Myung Moon*(Paragon House, MN. 2007) 222

65 Constance Victoria Brigges, *Encyclopedia of the Unseen World* (Weiser Books, S.F., 2010) 29

66 Harold Bloom, *Omens of Millennium* (Riverhead Books, New York, 1996) 40

67 Kerry Pobanz, *The Spirit Person and the Spirit-World* (HSA Publications, New York, 2001) 94

68 Mark H. Macy, *Miracle in the Storm* (New American Library, New York, 2001) 49

162

69   Kerry Pobanz, *The Spirit Person and the Spirit-World* (HSA Publications, New York, 2001) 71

70   Melvin Morse, MD., *Transformed by the Light* (Villard, New York, 1992) 163

71   Mark H. Macy, *Miracle in the Storm* (New American Library, New York, 2001) 79

72   Sun Myung Moon, *The Divine Principle* (HSA-UWC publications, New York, 1973) 76

73   Sylvia Brown, *Life on the Other Side* (Penguin Books, New York, 2001) 152

74   Arthur O. Roberts, *Exploring Heaven*, (Harper, San Francisco, 2003) 91

75   Lisa Miller, *Heaven, Our Enduring Fascination with the Afterlife* (Harper, New York, 2010) 161

76   David Fontana, *Life Beyond Death* (Watkins Publishing, London, 2009) 186

77   Sylvia Brown, *Life on the Other Side* (Penguin Books, New York, 2001) 95

78   Sylvia Brown, *Life on the Other Side* (Penguin Books, New York, 2001) 97

79   Dr. Jesse Herman Holmes, *As We See It From Here*(Metascience Corp.Publication, N.Carolina, 1980) 65

80   Mary T. Brown, *Life After Death* (Random House, NY, 1994) 70

81   Sun Myung Moon, *Cheon Seong Gyeong* (Sunghwa Publishing Company, 2006) 875

82   Borgia, Anthony, *Here and Hereafter* (Psychic Press Limited, London, 1968) 115

83   Sun Myung Moon, *Cheon Seong Gyeong* (Sunghwa Publishing Company, 2006) 859

84   Sun Myung Moon, *Cheon Seong Gyeong* (Sunghwa Publishing Company, 2006) 638

85   Borgia, Anthony, *Here and Hereafter* (Psychic Press Limited, London, 1968) 82

86   Borgia, Anthony, *Life in the World Unseen* (Psychic Press Limited, London, 1954) 43

87   Borgia, Anthony, *Here and Hereafter* (Psychic Press Limited, London, 1968) 126

88   Sun Myung Moon, *Cheon Seong Gyeong* (Sunghwa Publishing Company, 2006) 815

89   Sun Myung Moon, *Cheon Seong Gyeong* (Sunghwa Publishing Company, 2006) 856

90   Sylvia Brown, *Life on the Other Side* (Penguin Books, New York, 2001) 118

91   Mary T. Brown, *Life After Death* (Random House, NY, 1994) 73

92   Michael Talbot, *The Holographic Universe* (Harper Collins, New York, 1991) 272

93   Sang Han Lee, *Life in the Spirit World and on Earth* (Family Federation, 1998) 75

94   Sang Han Lee, *Life in the Spirit World and on Earth* (Family Federation, 1998) 17

95   Sun Myung Moon, *Cheon Seong Gyeong* (Sunghwa Publishing Company, 2006) 872

96   Anthony Borgia, *More About Life in the World Unseen* (Psychic Press Limited, London, UK) 75

97   Kerry Pobanz, *The Spirit Person and the Spirit World (HS A Publications, New York, 2001) 44*

98   Sun Myung Moon, *Cheon Seong Gyeong* (Sunghwa Publishing Company, 2006) 815

164

99 Universal Peace Federation,*World Scriptures & the Teachings—Sun Myung Moon*(Paragon House, MN. 2007) 208

100 Anthony Borgia, *Life in the World Unseen* (Psychic Press Limited, London, 1954) 155

HELL

101 David Fontana, *Life Beyond Death* (Watkins Publishing, London, 2009) 100

102 Bill Weise, *23 Minutes in Hell* (Charisma House, Florida, 2005) 33

103 Robert A. Monroe, *Ultimate Journey* (Doubleday, New York, 1994) 128

104 Bill Weise, *23 Minutes in Hell* (Charisma House, Florida, 2005) 7-13

105 Kerry Pobanz, *The Spirit Person and the Spirit World (HS A Publications, New York, 2001) 43*

106 Anthony Borgia, *Life in the World Unseen* (Psychic Press Limited, London, 1954) 127

107 Franchezzo, *Wanderer in the Spirit Worlds* (Aim Publishing, West Grove, PA. 1993) 25

108 Sylvia Brown, *Life on the Other Side* (Penguin Books, New York, 2001) 61

109 Kerry Pobanz, *The Spirit Person and the Spirit World (HS A Publications, New York, 2001) 44*

110 Anthony Borgia, *Life in the World Unseen* (Psychic Press Limited, London, 1954) 131

111 Anthony Borgia, *Life in the World Unseen* (Psychic Press Limited, London, 1954) 83

112 Bruce Moen, *Voyage to Curiosity's Father* (Hampton Roads, London,2001) 117

113   Franchezzo, *Wanderer in the Spirit World* (Aim Pubiliching, West Grove, PA.) 125

114   Anthony Borgia, *Life in the World Unseen* (Psychic Press Limited, London, 1954) 83

115   George W. Meek, *After We Die, What Then?* (Ariel Press, Columbus, Ohio,1987) 101

116   Sang Han Lee, *Life in the Spirit World and on Earth* (Family Federation, 1998) 17

117   David Fontana, *Life Beyond Death* (Watkins Publishing, London, 2009) 99

118   Sukie Miller, *After Death,* (Touchstone, New York , 1997) 127

119   Sukie Miller, *After Death,* (Touchstone, New York , 1997) 126

120   Franchezzo, *Wanderer in the Spirit World* (Aim Pubiliching, West Grove, PA.) 147

121   Deepak Chopra, *Life After Death* (Harmony Books, New York, 2006) 73

122   http://new-birth.net/booklet/GettingOut.PDF

123   Universal Peace Federation,*World Scriptures & the Teachings—Sun Myung Moon*(Paragon House, MN. 2007)217

124   Mary T. Brown, *Life After Death* (Random House, NY, 1994) 92

125   Mary T. Brown, *Life After Death* (Random House, NY, 1994) 96

126   Ptolemy Tompkins, *The Modern Book of the Dead* (Atria Books, New York, 2012) 30

127   Sang Han Lee, *Life in the Spirit World and on Earth* (Family Federation, 1998) 26

166

128 Sun Myung Moon, *Cheon Seong Gyeong* (Sunghwa Publishing Company, 2006) 824

129 Sun Myung Moon, *Cheon Seong Gyeong* (Sunghwa Publishing Company, 2006) 849

130 Franchezzo, *Wanderer in the Spirit World* (Aim Pubiliching, West Grove, PA.) 150

131 Franchezzo, Wanderer in the Spirit Worlds (Aim Publishing, West Grove, PA. 1993) 28

132 Sang Han Lee, *Life in the Spirit World and on Earth* (Family Federation, 1998) 75

133 George W. Meek, *After We Die, What Then?* (Ariel Press, Columbus, Ohio,1987) 104

134 Anthony Borgia, *Life in the World Unseen* (Psychic Press Limited, London, 1954) 132

135 Universal Peace Federation,*World Scriptures & the Teachings—Sun Myung Moon*(Paragon House, MN. 2007)184

136 Sharon L. Baker, *Razing Hell* (Westminister Knox Press, Louisville, KY., 2010) 64

137 Sun Myung Moon, *Divine Principle* (HSA Publications, New York, 1973) 228

138 http://new-birth.net/booklet/GettingOut.PDF

MEDIUMS
139 Pamela Rae Heath and Jon Klimo, *Handbook of the Afterlife* (North Atlantic Books, Berkeley, CA.2010) 50

140 Migene Gonzalez-Wippler, What *Happens After Death* (Llewellyn Publications, MN. 1997) 99

141 Elizabeth Lloyd Mayer, Ph.D., *Extraordinary Knowing* (Bantan Books, New York, 2007) 74

142   Peter K. Aykroyd, *A History of Ghosts*, (Rodale, New York, 2009) 88

143   Peter K. Aykroyd, *A History of Ghosts*, (Rodale, New York, 2009) 84

144   Michael Talbot, *The Holographic Universe* (Harper Collins, New York, 1991) 176

145   Michael Talbot, *The Holographic Universe* (Harper Collins, New York, 1991) 176

146   Michael Talbot, *The Holographic Universe* (Harper Collins, New York, 1991) 145

147   Michael Talbot, *The Holographic Universe* (Harper Collins, New York, 1991) 172

148   Dr. Sally Rhine Feather, *The Gift* (St. Martins Paperbacks, New York, 2005) 268

149   Deborah Blum, *Ghost Hunters,* (Penguin Press, New York, 2006) 13

150   David Fontana, *Life Beyond Death* (Watkins Publishing, London, 2009) 145

151   Dr. Sally Rhine Feather, *The Gift* (St. Martins Paperbacks, New York, 2005) 247

152   Dr. Jesse Herman Holmes, *As We See It From Here* (Metascience Corp.Publication, N.Carolina, 1980) 89

153   Sidney D. Kirkpatrick, *Edgar Cayce, An American Prophet* (Riverhead Books, NY, 2000) 10

154   Mitch Horowitz, *Occult America,* (Bantam Books, New York, 2009) 37

155   Peter H. Aykroyd, *The History of Ghosts* (Rodale, New York, 2009) 11

156   Joseph McMoneagle, *The Ultimate Time Machine,* (Hampton Roads, Charlottesville, VA.,1998) 114

157   Larry Dorset, M.D., *The Power of Premonitions* (Dutton, New York, 2009) 98

158   Michael Talbot, *The Holographic Universe* (Harper Collins, New York, 1991) 209

159   Michael Talbot, *The Holographic Universe* (Harper Collins, New York, 1991) 209

160   Larry Dorset, M.D., *The Power of Premonitions* (Dutton, New York, 2009) xx

161   Larry Dorset, M.D., *The Power of Premonitions* (Dutton, New York, 2009) 9

162   Robert Moss, *Dreamgates, Exploring the Worlds of the Soul, Imagination, and Life Beyond Death* (New World Library, Novato, CA. 2010) 50

163   Rob Macgregor, *Psychic Power* (Barrons, New York, 2005) 80

164   Michael Talbot, *The Holographic Universe* (Harper Collins, New York, 1991) 211

165   Michael Talbot, *The Holographic Universe* (Harper Collins, New York, 1991) 216

166   Larry Dorset, M.D., *The Power of Premonitions* (Dutton, New York, 2009) 84

167   Larry Dossey, M.D., *The Power of Premonitions* (Dutton, New York, 2009) 182

DREAMS
168   Universal Peace Federation, *World Scriptures and the Teachings of Sun Myung Moon* (Paragon House, MN. 2007) 194

169   George W. Meek, *After We Die, What Then?* (Ariel Press, Columbus, Ohio,1987) 122

170   Mary T. Brown, *Life After Death* (Random House, NY, 1994) 147

171   George W. Meek, *After We Die, What Then?* (Ariel Press, Columbus, Ohio,1987) 173

172   Robert Moss, *The Three Only Things, Tapping the Power of Dreams, Coincidence & Imagination*, (New World Library, CA., 2007) 41

173   Harold Sherman, *Your Live After Death*, (Merit Publications, New York, 1949) 171

174   Gayle Delaney, Ph.D., *All About Dreams*, (Harper, San Francisco, 1998) 228

175   Universal Peace Federation,*World Scriptures & the Teachings—Sun Myung Moon*(Paragon House, MN. 2007)192

176   Montague Ullman, M.D., *Dream Telepathy*, (Hampton Roads, VA.2001) 5

177   Thomas H. Flaherty, *The Spirit World*, (Time-Life, Alexandria, VA., 1992) 8

178   Harold Sherman, *Your Live After Death*, (Merit Publications, New York, 1949) 136

179   Michael Talbot, *The Holographic Universe* (Harper Collins, New York, 1991) 210

180   Mary T. Brown, *Life After Death*, (Random House, New York, 1994) 17

181   Thomas H. Flaherty, *The Spirit World*, (Time-Life, Alexandria, VA., 1992) 8

182   Thomas H. Flaherty, *The Spirit World*, (Time-Life, Alexandria, VA., 1992) 127

183   Patricia Garfield, Ph.D., *Creative Dreaming*, (Simon & Schuster, 1995) 84

184   Michael Talbot, *The Holographic Universe* (Harper Collins, New York, 1991) 65

170

185 Montague Ullman, M.D., *Dream Telepathy*, (Hampton Roads, VA.2001)184

186 Robert Moss, *Dreamgates* (New World, CA.,2010) 106

187 David Gordan, Ph.D. *Mindful Dreaming* (New Page Books, Franklin Lakes, NJ, 2007) 9

188 Sidney D. Kirkpatrick, *Edgar Cayce, An American Prophet* (Riverhead Books, NY, 2000) 353

189 Robert L. Van De Castle, Ph.D. *Our Dreaming Mind* (Ballantine Books, NY,1994) 39

190 Numbers 12:6

191 Sun Myung Moon, *The Will of God and Individual Perfection* (New York, HSA-UWC)

192 Acts 2: 17

193 Matthew 27:19

194 Gayle Delaney, Ph.D., *All About Dreams*, (Harper, San Francisco, 1998) 48

195 Brian Innes, *The Book of Dreams* (Gramercy Books, New York,2000) 26

196 Peter Farb, *Man's Rise to Civilization*(E.P. Dutton, New York, 1978) 160

197 Robert Moss, *Dreamgates*(New World, CA.,2010) 110

198 John A. Sanford, *Dreams, God Forgotten Language* (Harper, San Francisco, 1989) 43

199 Robert L.Van De Castle *Our Dreaming Mind*, (Ballantine Books, New York, 1994) 64

200 Anthony Borgia, *Life in the World Unseen* (Psychic Press Limited, London, 1954) 177

201 Robert Moss, *The Three Only Things, Tapping the Power of Dreams, Coincidence & Imagination*, (New World Library, CA., 2007) 60

202   Do you get Inspiration from Dreams? At http://tech-nocrat.net/d/2006/10/5/8694/

203   Robert Moss, *The Secret History of Dreaming*, (New World, CA., 2009) 123

204   Robert Moss, *The Three Only Things, Tapping the Power of Dreams, Coincidence & Imagination*, (New World Library, CA., 2007) 65

205   Larry Dorset, M.D., *The Power of Premonitions* (Dutton, New York, 2009) 98

206   Anthony Borgia, *Life in the World Unseen* (Psychic Press Limited, London, 1954) 154

207   Pamela Rae Heath & Jon Klimo, *Handbook of the Afterlife* (North Atlantic Books, Berkeley, CA, 2010) 199

208   Pamela Rae Heath & Jon Klimo, *Handbook of the Afterlife* (North Atlantic Books, Berkeley, CA, 2010) 194

209   Robert Moss, *Dreamgates* (New World, CA.,2010) 44

210   Robert Moss, *Dreamgates* (New World, CA.,2010) 273

211   Migene Gonzalez-Wippler, *What Happens After Death* (Llewellyn Publications, MN. 1997) 84

212   Robert Moss, *Dreamgates* (New World, CA.,2010) 12

213   Mary T. Brown, *Life After Death* (Random House, NY, 1994) 162

214   Montague Ullman, M.D., *Dream Telepathy*, (Hampton Roads, VA.2001) 21

215   Rob Macgregor, *Psychic Power* (Barrons, New York, 2005) 128

TRANSCOMMUNICATION

216   George W. Meek, *After We Die, What Then?* (Ariel Press, Columbus, Ohio,1987) 12

217 Michael Talbot, *The Holographic Universe* (Harper Collins, New York, 1991) 54

218 Migene Gonzalez-Wippler, *What Happens After Death* (Llewellyn Publications, MN. 1997) 17

219 Mark H. Macy, *Miracle in the Storm* (New American Library, New York, 2001) 114

220 Mark H. Macy, *Miracle in the Storm* (New American Library, New York, 2001) 57

221 Anabela Cardoso, *Electronic Voices* (Winchester, U.K., 2010) 92

222 Mark H. Macy, *Miracle in the Storm* (New American Library, New York, 2001) 42

223 Anabela Cardoso, *Electronic Voices* (Winchester, U.K., 2010) 101

224 Anthony Borgia, *Life in the World Unseen* (Psychic Press Limited, London, 1954) 162

225 Sun Myung Moon, *Cheon Seong Gyeong* (Sunghwa Publishing Company, 2006) 919

226 Migene Gonzalez-Wippler, *What Happens After Death* (Llewellyn Publications, MN. 1997) 98

227 Anabela Cardoso, *Electronic Voices* (Winchester, U.K., 2010) 169

228 George W. Meek, *After We Die, What Then?* (Ariel Press, Columbus, Ohio,1987) 172

229 Peter H. Aykroyd, *A History of Ghosts* (Rodale, New York, 2009) 114

230 Harold Sherman, *Your Live After Death* (Merit Publications, New York, 1949) 138

231 Harold Sherman, *Your Live After Death* (Merit Publications, New York, 1949) 194

232   George W. Meek, *After We Die, What Then?* (Ariel Press, Columbus, Ohio,1987) 96

REINCARNATION

233   Kerry Pobanz, *The Spirit Person and the Spirit-World* (HSA Publications, New York, 2001) 130

234   Jim B. Tucker, M.D., *Life Before Life* (St.Martins Press, New York, 2005) 4

235   Sun Myung Moon, *Cheon Seong Gyeong* (Sunghwa Publishing Company, 2006) 911

236   Sukie Miller, *After Death,* (Touchstone, New York , 1997) 144

237   George W. Meek, *After We Die, What Then?* (Ariel Press, Columbus, Ohio,1987) 131

238   George W. Meek, *After We Die, What Then?* (Ariel Press, Columbus, Ohio,1987) 184

239   Pamela Rae Heath & Jon Klimo, *Handbook of the After-life* (North Atlantic Books, Berkeley, CA, 2010) 154

240   Ptolemy Tompkins, *The Modern Book of the Dead* (Atria Books, New York, 2012) 74

241   Jim B. Tucker, M.D., *Life Before Life* (St.Martins Press, New York, 2005) 196

242   Kerry Pobanz, *The Spirit Person and the Spirit-World* (HSA Publications, New York, 2001) 151

243   Kerry Pobanz, *The Spirit Person and the Spirit-World* (HSA Publications, New York, 2001) 129

244   Kerry Pobanz, *The Spirit Person and the Spirit-World* (HSA Publications, New York, 2001) 157

245   Michael Talbot, *The Holographic Universe* (Harper Collins, New York, 1991) 68

174

246   Kerry Pobanz, *The Spirit Person and the Spirit-World* (HSA Publications, New York, 2001) 136

247   David Fontana, *Life Beyond Death* (Watkins Publishing, London, 2009) 122

248   Kerry Pobanz, *The Spirit Person and the Spirit-World* (HSA Publications, New York, 2001) 141

249   Mary T. Brown, *Life After Death*, (Random House, New York, 1994) 44

250   Sidney D. Kirkpatrick, *Edgar Cayce, An American Prophet* (Riverhead Books, NY, 2000) 256

251   Brian L. Weiss, M.D., *Many Lives, Many Masters* (Fireside Book, New York, 1988) 85

252   Kerry Pobanz, *The Spirit Person and the Spirit-World* (HSA Publications, New York, 2001) 154

253   Universal Peace Federation, *World Scriptures & the Teachings-Sun Myung Moon* (Paragon House,MN.2007) 227

254   Sun Myung Moon, *The Divine Principle* (HSA-UWC publications, New York, 1973) 182

255   Universal Peace Federation,*World Scriptures & the Teachings-Sun Myung Moon* (Paragon House, MN. 2007) 230

256   Sun Myung Moon, *The Divine Principle* (HSA-UWC publications, New York, 1973) 188

CONCLUSION

257   Napoleon Hill, *Outwitting the Devil* (Sterling Publishing, New York, 2011) 83

258   Borgia, Anthony, *Life in the World Unseen* (Psychic Press Limited, London, 1954) 163

259   Michael Talbot, *The Holographic Universe* (Harper Collins, New York, 1991) 244

260   Kerry Pobanz, *The Spirit Person and the Spirit-World* (HSA Publications, New York, 2001) 68

261   Sun Myung Moon, *The Divine Principle* (HSA-UWC publications, New York, 1973) 169

262   Dr. Jesse Herman Holmes, *As We See It From Here* (Metascience Corp.Publication, N.Carolina, 1980) 53

263   Migene Gonzalez-Wippler, *What Happens After Death* (Llewellyn Publications, MN. 1997) 85

264   Universal Peace Federation,*World Scriptures & the Teachings-Sun Myung Moon* (Paragon House, MN. 2007) 179

265   Anthony Borgia, *Here and Hereafter* (Psychic Press Limited, London, 1968) 12

266   Anthony Borgia, *Life in the World Unseen* (Psychic Press Limited, London, 1954) 160

267   Deepak Chopra, *Life After Death* (Harmony Books, New York, 2006) 26

268   Robert A. Monroe, *Ultimate Journey* (Doubleday, New York,1994) 258

269   Jeffrey Long, M.D., *Evidence of the Afterlife* (Harper One, New York, 2010) 3

270   Dr. Jesse Herman Holmes, *As We See It From Here*(Metascience Corp.Publication, N.Carolina, 1980) 102

271   Mary T. Brown, *Life After Death* (Random House, NY, 1994) 175

272   Michael Talbot, *The Holographic Universe* (Harper Collins, New York, 1991) 299

176

EPILOGUE

273   Mary T. Brown, *Life After Death* (Random House, NY, 1994) 112

274   Sun Myung Moon, *Cheon Seong Gyeong* (Sunghwa Publishing Company, 2006) 802

275   Deepak Chopra, *Life After Death* (Harmony Books, New York, 2006) 8

276   Kerry Pobanz, *The Spirit Person and the Spirit-World* (HSA Publications, New York, 2001) 180

277   Pamela Rae Heath and Jon Klimo, *Handbook of the Afterlife* (North Atlantic Books, Berkeley, CA.2010) 106

278   George W. Meek, *After We Die, What Then?* (Ariel Press, Columbus, Ohio,1987) 105

279   Mary T. Brown, *Life After Death* (Random House, NY, 1994) 134